atlanta

125 Recipes From 25 Top Atlanta Chefs

cooks

MELISSA LIBBY

FOOD PHOTOGRAPHY BY JOEY IVANSCO
BLACK & WHITE PHOTOGRAPHY BY TIM WILKERSON

LONGSTREET PRESS

Atlanta

atlanta

125 Recipes From 25 Top Atlanta Chefs

cooks

Published by
LONGSTREET PRESS, INC.
2974 Hardman Court
Atlanta, Georgia 30305

Printed in the United States of America

1st printing 2001

Library of Congress Catalog Card Number: 2001096672

ISBN: 1-56352-692-1

Jacket and book design by Burtch Hunter Design

A portion of the proceeds from the sale of *Atlanta Cooks* will be donated to Project Open Hand, an organization that brings nutritious and good-tasting meals to people who might otherwise go hungry.

Wholly committed to the mission of providing food for those in need, Project Open Hand is the only agency in Atlanta providing nutrition services to people with AIDS and other critical illnesses under the age of 60. The highly dedicated staff, with a base of more than 1,500 active volunteers of all ages, incomes and backgrounds, joins together to keep labor costs at a minimum, enabling Project Open Hand to pass on high-quality, lovingly prepared meals to those they serve.

Since 1988, Project Open Hand has never missed a day of delivery, never maintained a waiting list and never denied service to anyone meeting eligibility requirements.

ACKNOWLEDGMENTS

Atlanta Cooks began as a small, spiral-bound recipe collection and blossomed into the book you hold in your hands. I quickly realized that I was going to need help... and lots of it! Joey Ivansco, a longtime friend and highly acclaimed photographer, was invaluable, carefully orchestrating each food photo and making sure that each one met his high personal standards. His partner in this endeavor was food stylist Sara Levy. I watched in amazement as she made a beautiful dish look even better — time after time. Tim Wilkerson, a real gem and master of black & white photography, went to each restaurant at its busiest hour to catch the chef in action. His creativity and enthusiasm make the black & white photos a priceless addition to this book. Then there were 125 recipes to test and format. Led by Maureen C. Petrosky, the recipe team of Gena Berry, Gloria Smiley and Steve Rooney shopped, cooked, tweaked, recooked, and then had lots of dinner parties for friends willing to be tasters! And finally, the nitty-gritty work went to three members of my fabulous staff: Nicole Robinson, Gretchen Schorer and Catie Woods. They set and supervised photo shoots, secured and organized the recipes, wrote copy and kept it fun with their enthusiasm for the project. They made it happen.

INTRODUCTION

As recently as ten years ago, the only recipe people were clamoring for in Atlanta was the secret formula to Coca-Cola. We still don't know the special ingredients behind that classic product, but the quest for great Atlanta recipes has definitely expanded. Those of us who have lived in Atlanta long enough have watched its transformation from a pleasant, small-town atmosphere to a bustling metropolis with sophistication, culture, diversity and an appetite for excellent dining experiences. The great chefs soon followed, savoring the opportunity to build their dreams in a city of opportunity, hospitality and beauty. Not one of the restaurants in this book was open before 1990. Today, there are enough top chefs in this city to fill several editions of *Atlanta Cooks*.

Certainly Atlanta is known for traditional Southern food, but innovative restaurant chefs creating delicious cuisines of all types have put the culinary spotlight on the city. National magazine writers and television producers now put it on their list of places to visit for great food. Atlanta truly has become a dining destination.

The chefs featured in *Atlanta Cooks* are sharing some of their best dishes. They each took the time to write the recipe for the home cook, reducing portion size and substituting hard-to-find ingredients with more readily available ones. The community of chefs is still small and convivial, and they relish the opportunity to showcase their talents together for the good of the city.

Every chef featured has made his or her mark on Atlanta. Most have won awards for their talents. Many have been featured in national publications. All turn out mouthwatering dishes. In the spirit that defines the Atlanta restaurant community, they are sharing these recipes willingly and cheerfully — because you are their guests, and they want to please you.

Here's to a great dinner, y'all!

atlanta

125 Recipes From 25 Top Atlanta Chefs

cooks

FOOD 101

CHEF SCOTT CRAWFORD

Serving hearty food with rural roots and an urban polish, Food 101 caters to those seeking a dining experience reminiscent of days gone by. Created by talented chef Scott Crawford, the menu features proven classics with an inventive twist. Comparable to a traditional, 1920s New York speak-easy, the Sandy Springs eatery exudes comfort not only through its food, but also through its relaxed atmosphere.

YANKEE POT ROAST WITH BRAISED VEGETABLES

1 eye of round or other beef suitable for braising
3 cloves garlic, mashed to a paste
2 tablespoons chili powder
1 lemon, zest and juice
Kosher salt
Freshly ground black pepper
2 tablespoons oil
1 ½ cups red wine

2 yellow onions, quartered
2 ribs celery, cut into 1" pieces
2 carrots, peeled and cut into 1" pieces
2 shallots, peeled and quartered
4-5 cups veal stock (beef stock may be substituted)
2 tablespoons flour
1 tablespoon milk

Rub the beef with the garlic, chili powder and lemon, cover or put in a Ziploc bag, refrigerate and let marinate for at least 8 hours. Just before you are ready to cook the meat, season with salt and pepper. In a large, straight-sided sauté pan with lid, heat the oil and sear the beef on all sides to seal in the juices. When all sides are nicely browned, add the red wine to de-glaze the pan and scrape up all the browned bits. Add the vegetables and cook until lightly browned. Add the stock to cover the meat and vegetables. Return to a boil, then reduce the heat to a low simmer, cover and cook for 4 hours or until tender.

Remove the meat from the pot and let rest. Remove the vegetables and keep warm. To thicken the gravy, stir the flour and milk together and whisk into the braising liquid. Cook for about 5 minutes until nicely thickened. Plate some vegetables and sliced pot roast, and top with the gravy.

Serves 8

GRILLED SAGE CHICKEN WITH THREE-POTATO HASH

Chicken
3 tablespoons fresh sage
½ cup olive oil
¼ cup Pommery/whole grain mustard
Salt and freshly ground black pepper
6 boneless breasts, wing tips attached

Hash
2 tablespoons vegetable oil
1 cup red onion, cut into large dice
4 new potatoes, washed and cut into small dice
1 small-to-medium Idaho potato, washed and cut into small dice
4 purple Peruvian potatoes, washed and cut into small dice
¼ cup Pommery/whole grain mustard
2 cups chicken stock
4 teaspoons fresh sage, chopped
Kosher salt
Freshly ground black pepper

For the chicken, mix the sage, oil and mustard together and season with salt and pepper. Gently pound the chicken to even out the thickness. Marinate the chicken in sage mixture for 1 hour. Grill chicken, skin-side first, 6 minutes per side or until cooked through. You may partially cook and finish in the oven.

For the hash, in a large sauté pan, heat the oil. Add the diced onion and cook until nicely browned and caramelized, about 15 minutes. Add the potatoes and cook over high heat for about 5 minutes. Fold in the mustard and ½ cup stock. Continue cooking and adding stock a little at a time until the potatoes are cooked through, about 10-15 more minutes. Fold in the sage and generously season to taste with salt and pepper.

Plate a serving of hash and top with a chicken breast.

Serves 6

MEATLOAF WITH YUKON GOLD MASHED POTATOES AND RED WINE GRAVY

Meatloaf
1½ pounds ground beef
1½ pounds Italian sausage, casings removed
1 small onion, julienned
3 eggs
2 teaspoons kosher salt
1 teaspoon freshly ground black pepper
2 cloves garlic, minced
½ cup ketchup
1 teaspoon cayenne pepper
1 teaspoon paprika
1½ cups bread crumbs

Gravy
2 tablespoons oil
1 small onion, chopped
2 ribs celery, chopped
1 carrot, chopped
2 cloves garlic, minced
½ cup tomato paste
1 750-ml bottle red wine
6 cups veal or beef stock
3 tablespoons flour
Kosher salt
Freshly ground black pepper

Potatoes
2 pounds Yukon gold potatoes
8 tablespoons butter
¾ cup milk
2 teaspoons kosher salt
1 teaspoon freshly ground black pepper

Preheat oven to 350°. For the meatloaf, in a large mixing bowl, mix the ground beef, sausage and onion. In a small bowl, beat the eggs and add to the meat mixture. Mix together the salt, pepper, garlic, ketchup, cayenne and paprika. Stir into the meat mixture. Stir in the bread crumbs. Form into 2 loaves and place on a sheet pan. Bake for about 1 hour, or until cooked through and the internal temperature reaches 160°. Cooking time will be dependent upon the size and shape of the loaves.

For the gravy, in a large, heavy-bottomed pot, sauté the vegetables and garlic in the oil until caramelized. Add the tomato paste and cook until a dark-brown color. Be careful not to burn. Add the wine and reduce until thick. Add the stock and reduce by half, or until the flavor is deep and rich. Make a slurry by mixing the flour with 2 tablespoons water until smooth. Strain the gravy and return to the pan and thicken with the slurry. Season to taste with salt and pepper.

For the potatoes, boil the potatoes in a large pot of salted water until tender and skins are cracked. Drain. Cut the butter into small cubes and mash together with the potatoes and milk. Season to taste with salt and pepper.

Serves 8

CHICKEN SOUP

¼ cup canola or vegetable oil
1½ pounds boneless, skinless chicken (breasts and/or thighs)
4 cloves garlic, chopped
1 cup celery, diced
1 cup onion, diced
½ cup carrots, diced
1½ tablespoons fresh thyme, minced
1 tablespoon fresh oregano, minced
12 cups chicken stock
Juice of one lemon
Kosher salt
Freshly ground black pepper

In a large stockpot, heat the oil. Dice the chicken and stir into the oil. Cook the chicken for 5 minutes, stir-ring often. Add the garlic and cook for 2 more minutes. Add the celery, onion and carrots and cook until they are tender and the onions are translucent, about 10 minutes. Add the thyme, oregano and stock and bring to a boil. Reduce the heat and skim the soup, removing any fat and foam. Simmer the soup until reduced to two-thirds its original volume, or about 8 cups. Add the lemon juice and season to taste with salt and pepper.

Serves 6 to 8

GRILLED PEARS WITH CANDIED PECANS AND MIXED LETTUCES

1 cup water
1 cup sugar
1 cup pecans
⅓ cup balsamic vinegar
2 teaspoons fresh oregano, minced
1 teaspoon shallots, minced
1 teaspoon sugar
1 tablespoon chives, minced
1 tablespoon red onion, minced
1 cup canola oil
4 pears, ripe (d'Anjou work well)
3 tablespoons olive oil
Kosher salt
Freshly ground black pepper
5 cups spring mix/mesclun mix
3 ounces crumbled blue cheese (¼ cup)

Preheat oven to 350°. For the pecans, place the sugar and water in a small saucepan and bring to a boil. Add pecans and let simmer 5 minutes. Drain and toast the pecans on a well-greased baking sheet until golden, about 10 minutes. Set aside to cool.

For the dressing, in a small bowl, mix the vinegar with the oregano, shallots, sugar, chives and onion. Slowly whisk in the canola oil to form an emulsion. Taste and season with salt and pepper. Set aside.

For the pears, cut the pears in quarters and remove the seeds. Toss with olive oil and season with salt and pepper. Grill on a hot grill until marks start to appear. Set aside.

Toss the salad with the dressing and mound in the center of each plate. Place 4 pears around the greens and top with candied pecans and crumbled blue cheese.

Serves 4

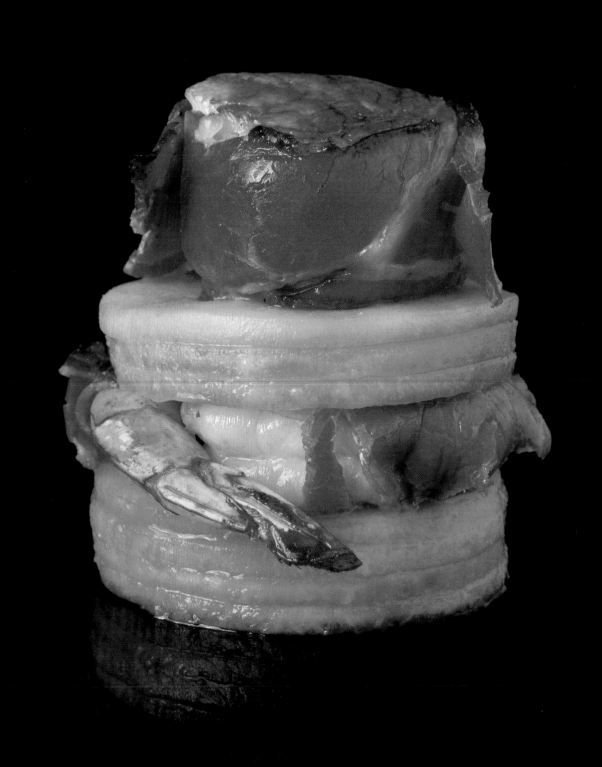

SOHO

CHEF JOE AHN

SoHo, a restaurant with décor reminiscent of New York's popular district of the same name, features bold, eclectic American cuisine. Chef Joe Ahn uses only the freshest ingredients to create the Vinings restaurant's light, focused menu. With a celebrated, consumer-friendly wine list and interactive wine tastings coupled with Ahn's delectable menu, SoHo is a popular spot for a night out in Atlanta.

PROSCIUTTO-WRAPPED SHRIMP AND SCALLOPS WITH TWO MELON SAUCES

8 jumbo shrimp
8 jumbo scallops
8 thinly sliced pieces of prosciutto, sliced in half lengthwise to get 16 pieces
¹/₂ cantaloupe
¹/₂ honeydew
¹/₄ cup olive oil
Salt and pepper to taste

Peel and devein shrimp. Remove muscle from scallops. Wrap each shrimp and each scallop individually in prosciutto. Reserve in the refrigerator.

Cut half of both the honeydew and the cantaloupe into chunks. Slice the remainder of each. Process the chunks of each separately in a blender until smooth.

In a large sauté pan over high heat, add enough oil to coat the pan. Sear the prosciutto-wrapped shrimp and scallops on each side. Drain on paper towels.

Place 2 shrimp and 2 scallops on top of slices of the cantaloupe and honeydew. Sauce each plate with both sauces.

Serves 4

APPLE CIDER BEET SALAD

4 red beets, peeled and quartered
1 quart apple cider or juice
½ cup red wine vinegar
½ cup walnuts
¼ cup granulated sugar
½ pound baby arugula or spinach
Juice of 1 lemon
¼ cup extra virgin olive oil
Salt and freshly ground black pepper to taste
½ cup blue cheese

In a medium saucepan, combine beets, apple cider and red wine vinegar. Simmer until beets are fork tender. Remove beets and juice from heat and chill together.

In a sauté pan, add walnuts and sugar and stir over medium heat until sugar turns a golden brown. Pour onto a greased cookie sheet to cool.

In a large bowl, mix the arugula, lemon juice, olive oil and salt and pepper. Plate the arugula and top with sliced beets, blue cheese and candied walnuts.

Serves 6 to 8

CHILEAN SEA BASS

Sauce
1 red bell pepper, seeded and cut into large dice
1 yellow bell pepper, seeded and cut into large dice
1 serrano pepper, seeded and roughly chopped
1 small yellow onion, cut into large dice
½ cup rice wine vinegar
½ cup water
Salt and freshly ground black pepper

Rice
¼ cup roasted sesame oil
2 tablespoons fresh ginger, minced
2 tablespoons garlic, minced
4 cups cooked Jasmine rice
½ cup chopped scallions
¼ cup soy sauce

4-6 7-ounce portions of Chilean sea bass
1 cup flour

For the sauce, in a small saucepan, add all ingredients and bring to a boil. Reduce heat and simmer for 15 minutes. Transfer to a food processor or blender and process until smooth. Strain through a fine mesh strainer and keep warm.

For the rice, in a nonstick pan over high heat, add sesame oil, ginger and garlic. Add rice and scallions and stir continually until rice is hot. Finish with soy sauce.

For the fish, preheat oven to 350°. Lightly salt and pepper each portion of the sea bass and dredge in flour. In a sauté pan over high heat, sear each side and finish cooking in the oven for 10-12 minutes.

Serve each piece of fish over rice with a topping of the sauce.

Serves 4 to 6

GOLDEN TOMATO GAZPACHO

4 large ripe golden tomatoes (peeled and seeded if preferred), roughly chopped
1 cucumber, peeled, seeded and roughly chopped
Juice of 1 lime
1 jalapeño, seeded and roughly chopped
¼ bunch cilantro
¼ cup finely diced red onion
¼ cup finely diced red bell pepper
Salt and pepper to taste

In a food processor blend tomatoes, cucumber, lime juice, jalapeño and cilantro until smooth. Season with salt and pepper.

Serve in a bowl and garnish with red onion and red bell pepper.

Serves 6

TUNA TARTARE AND AVOCADO NAPOLEON
WITH REDUCED BALSALMIC VINEGAR

2 cups balsamic vinegar
1 pound sushi-grade tuna
2 ripe avocados, peeled, pitted and thinly sliced
3 tablespoons fresh lime juice
2 cloves garlic, minced
2 teaspoons soy sauce
2 teaspoons toasted sesame oil
Salt and freshly ground black pepper

In a small saucepan over low heat, reduce the balsamic vinegar to ½ cup and set aside to cool.

In a large bowl, mix together all ingredients except avocado and balsamic reduction.

Line a coffee cup with plastic wrap. Spoon in 1 tablespoon of tuna mixture, then a layer of avocado, and repeat until you have three layers. Press down. Remove whole stack and flip onto a plate. Remove plastic wrap and garnish with balsamic reduction.

Serves 4

C A N O E

CHEF GARY L. MENNIE

One of the most influential dining venues in the great, green Southern city of Atlanta is Canoe. Since 1995, this unique restaurant on the banks of the Chattahoochee has been building a reputation for excellence. The spectacular location, exceptional cuisine and knowledgeable staff make Canoe extraordinary. Chef Gary L. Mennie features only the freshest seafood, farm-raised poultry and organic products brought in from local farms.

GREEN BEAN AND SHELLFISH SUCCOTASH WITH GRILLED CORN

1 pound green beans
¾ cup baby butter beans
Kosher salt
½ cup tomato concasse
2 tablespoons olive oil
1 small red onion, julienned
1 red pepper, cut into small dice
1 yellow pepper, cut into small dice
1 teaspoon garlic, minced
1 cup grilled corn
2 cups shellfish stock
2 tablespoons green onions, minced

In a large pot of boiling water, blanch the green beans for about 4 minutes and remove to an ice-water bath. Set aside. Cook the butter beans in a small amount of salted water until tender, about 15 minutes. In a medium saucepan, heat the oil and sauté onion, peppers and garlic. Add the green beans, butter beans and corn and sauté for another 3 minutes. Add the tomatoes and shellfish stock and cook another 2 minutes. Season with salt and pepper to taste and garnish with the green onions.

Serves 6

BLUE LAKE BEAN AND WILD MUSHROOM SALAD
WITH ROASTED CHESTNUTS

1 pound Blue Lake beans (or haricots verts)
2 tablespoons olive oil
1 pound assorted wild mushrooms (such as morels, porcini, matsutake)
1 tablespoon shallots, minced
1 teaspoon garlic, minced
½ cup fresh chestnuts, roughly chopped
2 teaspoons fresh sage, minced
1 tablespoon parsley, minced
Kosher salt
Freshly ground white pepper
1 tablespoon sherry wine vinegar

Fill a large pot with water and add 1 teaspoon salt. Bring the water to a boil and blanch the beans about 4 minutes or until tender. Immediately shock the beans in an ice-water bath. Remove the beans when cool, drain and set aside. In a large sauté pan, heat the oil and sauté the mushrooms for 3 minutes. Add the shallots and garlic and sauté for another 2 minutes. Add the blanched beans and chopped chestnuts and heat through. Add the herbs and season to taste with salt and pepper. Splash with the sherry vinegar and serve warm.

Serves 8

SMOKED SALMON WITH EGGPLANT CAVIAR
AND CITRUS-CAPER VINAIGRETTE

2 medium Italian eggplants
Kosher salt
2 tablespoons extra virgin olive oil, divided
2 red bell peppers
2 lemons
1 tablespoon capers
1 tablespoon shallots, minced
2 plum tomatoes, seeded and cut into small dice
1 tablespoon champagne vinegar
Freshly ground black pepper
6 ounces premium smoked salmon, thinly sliced

Preheat oven to 350°. Slice the eggplants in half, season with salt and rub with 1 tablespoon olive oil. Place cut-side down on a baking sheet and roast for 35-40 minutes or until tender. Scoop the flesh out of the skin. Let drain in a colander for 10 minutes and purée in a food processor. Set aside. Roast the red peppers whole on a grill or on broil in the oven until skins are black on all sides. Place peppers in a bowl and cover with plastic wrap to steam and cool, about 15 minutes. Remove the skins, seeds and stems. Cut the peppers with a cookie cutter into 1½-inch circles. Set aside.

For the vinaigrette, zest the skin of the lemons and blanch the zest in boiling water for 2 minutes. Segment the lemons, removing all of the rind and membrane. In a small bowl, combine the lemon segments, zest, capers, shallots, tomatoes, remaining 2 tablespoons olive oil and champagne vinegar. Taste and season with salt and pepper as needed.

Divide the salmon evenly among 4 plates, covering as much of the bottom of the plate as possible. Place a teaspoon of the eggplant on the center of the salmon. Top the eggplant with a pepper round and repeat 2 more times (napoleon-style). Spoon citrus-caper vinaigrette around the plate.

Serves 4

VEGETABLE PAELLA

½ cup baby zucchini, sliced
½ cup pattypan squash, sliced
½ cup sunburst squash, sliced
½ cup baby carrots, sliced
½ cup French green beans
½ cup olive oil
1 red onion, cut into ¼-inch dice
2 tablespoons garlic, minced
1 fennel bulb, cut into ¼-inch dice
½ red bell pepper, diced
1½ cups basmati rice
3½ cups vegetable stock
¼ teaspoon saffron
½ cup cherry tomatoes
½ cup artichoke hearts, quartered
2 teaspoons fresh thyme, minced
2 teaspoons fresh oregano, minced
2 teaspoons fresh rosemary, minced
1 bay leaf

Blanch the squash, carrots and green beans by cooking in boiling water for 4 minutes. Shock in an ice-water bath and then set aside. In a large pan, heat the olive oil. Sauté the onion, garlic, fennel and pepper. Add the rice and stir to coat. Add the vegetable stock and saffron. Cook for 10 minutes and add sautéed vegetables. Cook for 10 more minutes and add the blanched vegetables, tomatoes, artichoke hearts and herbs. Simmer another 10 minutes, until all liquid is absorbed. Let rest 5 minutes before serving.

Serves 8

WILD MUSHROOM SOUP

8 cups chicken stock
½ cup dried cepes (porcini mushrooms)
¼ cup extra virgin olive oil
½ stalk celery, cut into medium dice
½ yellow onion, cut into medium dice
⅓ cup leeks, white part only, cut into medium dice
3 cloves garlic
2 shallots, cut into medium dice
1 cup julienned shiitake mushrooms
1 cup julienned cremini mushrooms
1 cup julienned portabello mushrooms
1 cup julienned chanterelle mushrooms
½ cup heavy cream
2 teaspoons sea salt
½ teaspoon freshly ground white pepper
1 teaspoon white truffle oil
Croutons for garnish

In a large pot, bring the chicken stock to a boil. Reduce heat and keep warm. Chop the cepes and reconstitute in 1 cup of the warm stock in a small bowl. Set aside. In a nonstick sauté pan, sauté celery, onions, leeks, garlic and shallots in 2 tablespoons oil until translucent. Set aside. Separately sauté each type of mushroom in a nonstick pan in a small amount of oil until they take on a golden color. Reserve ½ cup of cooked mushrooms for garnish. Put the sautéed onion mixture and all of the mushrooms including the cepes (including the stock they were reconstituted in) into the warm chicken stock. Return to a boil and reduce heat to simmer for 20 minutes. In a separate pot, heat the cream just to a simmer and add to the soup. Remove from the heat and let cool slightly. In small batches, purée the soup in a blender, being careful to leave the top loose so the steam can escape. Add salt, pepper and truffle oil. Taste and adjust final seasoning.

Enjoy topped with a garnish of the reserved sautéed mushrooms and some crusty olive oil-brushed croutons.

Serves 6

FIFTH GROUP RESTAURANTS

PASTRY CHEF GARY SCARBOROUGH

Responsible for the desserts offered at Atlanta favorites South City Kitchen, The Food Studio, La Tavola Trattoria and catering division Bold American Food Company, Pastry Chef Gary Scarborough is the icing on top of a highly successful restaurant group's cake. The dessert menus at these popular eateries receive much critical acclaim — pretty impressive considering Scarborough taught himself the fine craft.

LEMON BASIL BOMBE

¼ cup + 2 teaspoons freshly squeezed lemon juice, divided
¼ cup water
1 cup sugar
6 egg yolks
½ ounce fresh basil
2 cups heavy cream, whipped to soft peaks
Zest of 2 lemons
Vanilla ice cream, softened
Toasted coconut or graham cracker crumbs

Citrus Sauce
1 cup freshly squeezed orange juice, divided
2 tablespoons cornstarch
½ cup freshly squeezed grapefruit juice
½ cup freshly squeezed lemon juice
1½ tablespoons sugar

In a small saucepan, combine 2 teaspoons of lemon juice, water and sugar. Bring to a boil until syrup reads 240° on a candy thermometer. In a mixer, whip the egg yolks until thick and foamy. With the mixer still running, slowly add the lemon syrup down the side of the bowl. Continue mixing until cool.

In a food processor, combine basil, remaining lemon juice, and a few drops of water. Process until smooth. Fold this purée, the whipped cream and lemon zest into the egg-syrup mixture and refrigerate. Line a loaf pan with plastic wrap and make sure there are no air pockets. With a spatula, spread softened ice cream along the insides of the pan, about ¼-inch thick. Place in freezer until hardened. Once hardened, fill with bombe mixture and place back in freezer until frozen.

For the citrus sauce, in a small mixing bowl, combine 2 tablespoons of the orange juice with the cornstarch to make a thin paste with no lumps. Add the paste back to the rest of the orange juice. In a small nonreactive pot, combine orange juice, the remaining juices and sugar and bring to a boil for 2 minutes. Remove and strain. Chill.

Remove the bombe from freezer and dip the pan into warm water for 10 seconds. Pull the bombe out of the pan and remove the plastic wrap. Coat with toasted coconut or graham cracker crumbs. Slice and serve, or wrap in plastic wrap and keep in freezer for up to 2 weeks. Garnish each plate with citrus sauce.

Serves 8

CHOCOLATE CAKE WITH GANACHE FROSTING

Cake

1 cup brown sugar
1 cup sugar
1¾ cups cake flour
1 cup cocoa powder
1½ teaspoons baking powder
1½ teaspoons baking soda
½ teaspoon instant coffee
1 teaspoon salt
2 eggs
1 cup milk
½ cup melted butter
1 teaspoon vanilla
½ cup very hot water

Ganache

12 ounces good-quality dark chocolate
¾ cup + 1 tablespoon buttermilk
1 cup sour cream
¼ cup 10X powdered sugar

Preheat oven to 325°. Combine all dry ingredients and sift together in a large bowl. In a separate mixing bowl, add dry mixture, eggs, butter, milk and vanilla. Mix 3 minutes on medium speed. Scrape bowl once during mixing. Gradually add water. Fill 2 9-inch cake pans with mixture and bake for 35 minutes, or until a toothpick inserted in the middle comes out clean. Cool completely and frost with ganache.

For ganache, melt chocolate over a double boiler. In a separate pan, heat buttermilk, sour cream and sugar until warm. Mix milk mixture into chocolate. Stir until a spreading consistency. Use immediately or refrigerate. If frosting begins to stiffen, put in a microwave for 20 seconds to soften.

Serves 10 to 12

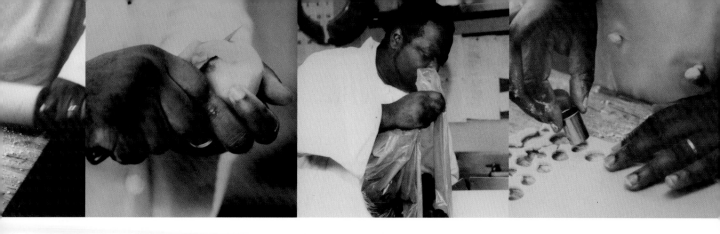

CHOCOLATE GOLD

1¼ cups heavy cream
½ cup sugar
3 tablespoons water
3 eggs, large
9 ounces good-quality dark chocolate
3 tablespoons butter, softened
1 8-ounce box chocolate wafer cookies

Ganache
12 ounces good-quality dark chocolate
¾ cup + 1 tablespoon buttermilk
1 cup sour cream
¼ cup 10X powdered sugar

Whip the cream to soft peaks and refrigerate. In a small saucepan, bring the sugar and water to a boil and cook until the mixture reads 250° on a candy thermometer. In a mixing bowl on second speed, whip the eggs until thick and foamy. Slowly add the sugar mixture, pouring down the side of the bowl. Continue mixing until eggs have tripled in size.

In a double boiler, melt the chocolate and the butter. When eggs are tripled in size, add to chocolate mixture. Then fold whipped cream into the chocolate mixture.

In a food processor, grind chocolate wafers until they are a coarse meal texture. Line a 10-inch springform pan with plastic wrap. Line the bottom of the pan with the ground cookies. Fill pan with chocolate mousse. Freeze overnight.

For ganache, melt chocolate over a double boiler. In a separate pan, heat buttermilk, sour cream and sugar until warm. Mix cream mixture into chocolate. Stir until a spreading consistency. Use immediately or refrigerate. If frosting begins to stiffen, put in a microwave for 20 seconds to soften.

Pull mousse from freezer and remove from pan. Remove plastic wrap and place the mousse on a cooling rack over a cookie sheet, wafer-side down. In an even motion, pour ganache over mousse to coat entire cake. Place in refrigerator for 20 minutes. Slice and serve.

Serves 12

MASCARPONE CHEESECAKE

Filling
2 8-ounce packages cream cheese
1 pound, 4 ounces mascarpone cheese
2 cups sugar
⅛ teaspoon salt
3 tablespoons cornstarch
¼ teaspoon vanilla extract
4 eggs
4 egg yolks
½ cup heavy cream
¼ cup + 1 tablespoon milk

Crust
1 stick butter
1 cup flour
1 cup sugar
1 cup ground hazelnuts

Preheat oven to 300°. In a mixing bowl, combine cream cheese and mascarpone cheese until smooth. Add sugar, salt and cornstarch. Scrape bowl. Continue mixing on low speed. Slowly add vanilla and eggs until completely combined. Add heavy cream and milk and combine. Set aside.

For the crust, in a food processor, combine butter, flour, sugar and ground hazelnuts. Line a 10½-inch springform pan with this mixture. Bake for 10 minutes. Remove and let cool.

Line outside of springform pan with aluminum foil. Add cheesecake filling. Place this pan in another pan large enough to act as a water bath. Fill the larger pan with water halfway up the sides of the springform pan. Place in 300° oven. Close the door and adjust temperature to 250°. Bake for 1 hour 40 minutes, or until cheesecake has completely set up. Remove from water bath and refrigerate at least 6 hours before serving.

Serves 12 to 16

CHOCOLATE PECAN PIE

Filling

1 cup dark brown sugar
¼ cup butter
¼ cup chocolate ganache
4 eggs
¾ bottle of dark corn syrup (1-pound bottle)
1½ tablespoons vanilla extract
1½ teaspoons rum
¼ cup chocolate chips
½ cup pecans, roughly chopped

Tart Dough

3 sticks unsalted butter, room temperature
⅓ cup + 1 tablespoon milk, room temperature
1 egg yolk, room temperature
1 teaspoon sugar
1 teaspoon salt
3 cups flour

For the filling, in a mixing bowl combine sugar, butter and ganache until smooth. Slowly add eggs until incorporated. Add corn syrup, vanilla and rum. Refrigerate.

For the dough, in a mixing bowl cream butter until smooth. Add milk, egg yolk, sugar and salt and beat until mixture is combined. Turn the mixer to low and add the flour in 3 stages. Mix until the dough is soft and won't stick to the sides of the bowl. Remove and place on a cutting board. Form the dough into 2 separate discs and cover with plastic wrap. Place 1 in the refrigerator and 1 in the freezer. Refrigerate at least 4 hours before using.

Preheat oven to 325°. Roll refrigerated dough to a circle large enough to cover a 9½-inch pie plate. Line tart dough with chocolate chips and pecans. Fill pie shell with filling, leaving ½ inch around the top. Bake for 1 hour 15 minutes, or until pie has completely set up.

Serves 8

SOUTH CITY KITCHEN

CHEF JAY SWIFT

Southern smiles and sophisticated tastes come together at South City Kitchen, a Midtown hotspot that has earned popular and critical acclaim since 1993 for merging traditional, regional ingredients with contemporary style. Chef Jay Swift oversees a menu of Southern favorites dressed up in novel ways. The dining room, housed in a renovated steel-and-glass bungalow, conveys the energy of a big city with the warmth of a neighborhood soul-food kitchen.

WARM ASPARAGUS SALAD WITH COUNTRY HAM AND GOLDEN TOMATOES

1 teaspoon Dijon mustard
1 shallot, minced
2 tablespoons cider vinegar
¼ cup vegetable oil
1 ounce country ham, julienned
12 spears thin asparagus
1 tablespoon Vidalia onion, sliced very thin
2 tablespoons tomato, seeded and diced
Kosher salt
Freshly ground black pepper
1 yellow tomato, sliced

For the vinaigrette, mix the mustard with the shallot and cider vinegar. Whisk in the vegetable oil. Season to taste with salt and pepper. Set aside.

In a sauté pan, gently warm the ham. Add the asparagus and onion and cook for 2 minutes. Toss in the red tomato and warm through. Add the vinaigrette and toss to coat. Taste and season with salt and pepper as needed.

Slice some yellow tomato onto the plate and top with the warm ham-asparagus salad.

Serves 4

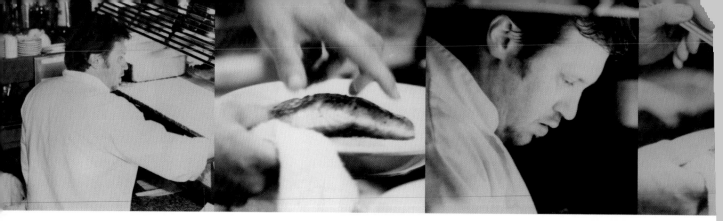

FRIED GREEN TOMATOES WITH GOAT CHEESE AND RED PEPPER COULIS

Coulis

3 red bell peppers, seeded and diced
½ large onion, diced
3 cloves garlic, minced
1 tablespoon olive oil
1 tablespoon sugar
¼ cup white wine
½ cup tomato juice
Kosher salt
6 fresh basil leaves, julienned
Freshly ground black pepper

Tomatoes

4 green tomatoes, sliced into ¼-inch slices
Salt and pepper to taste
½ cup flour
3 eggs
1 cup bread crumbs
4 cups canola oil for frying
5-6 ounces goat cheese, crumbled
Fresh basil for garnish

Sauté the peppers, onions and garlic in the olive oil until soft and the onions are translucent. Add the sugar and stir. Add white wine and reduce by half, about 3 minutes. Add the tomato juice and simmer gently for 20 minutes. Purée the pepper mixture in a blender until smooth. Strain through a fine mesh sieve, fold in the basil and season to taste with salt and pepper.

Preheat deep skillet with oil to 375°. Season the tomato slices generously with salt and pepper. Put the flour, eggs and crumbs in 3 separate flat bowls. Whisk the eggs. One at a time, dust both sides of the tomato slices with flour, dip in the egg and then coat with the bread crumbs. Deep-fry until golden brown, about 4 minutes. Drain on absorbent paper or paper towels.

Immediately arrange the drained tomatoes on a plate. Drizzle with the pepper coulis and sprinkle with the crumbled goat cheese. Garnish with a couple of fresh basil leaves.

Serves 6

SHE CRAB SOUP

4 tablespoons butter
1 cup yellow onion, roughly chopped
¼ cup celery, roughly chopped
⅓ cup flour
4 cups clam juice
2 tablespoons sherry
2 tablespoons white wine
½ teaspoon kosher salt
¼ teaspoon Tabasco sauce
½ teaspoon Worcestershire sauce
¼ teaspoon nutmeg
¼ teaspoon freshly ground white pepper
¼ teaspoon Old Bay seasoning
6 sprigs fresh thyme
1 bay leaf
4 cups whole milk
2 cups heavy cream
¼ pound lump or backfin crabmeat
⅛ pound crab roe, if available

Melt the butter in a large pot. Add the onion and celery and cook until soft and translucent, about 5 minutes. Stir in the flour, reduce heat and cook 5 minutes. Slowly stir in the clam juice, sherry and white wine. Cook over low heat 20 minutes. Add salt, Tabasco, Worcestershire, nutmeg, pepper, Old Bay, thyme and the bay leaf. Stir to blend. Stir in the milk and cream and simmer for 20 minutes, stirring occasionally. Strain the soup. Just before serving, add the crab and garnish each cup/bowl with the roe.

Serves 12

SKILLET-SEARED CRAB CAKES WITH WHOLE GRAIN MUSTARD

Mustard Sauce
1 teaspoon whole grain mustard
1 tablespoon chives, chopped
3 tablespoons crème fraîche

Crab Cakes
¼ cup mayonnaise
1 egg
Juice of 2 lemons
½ teaspoon Worcestershire sauce
1 tablespoon Old Bay seasoning
Kosher salt
Freshly ground black pepper
1 pound jumbo lump blue crabmeat
4 slices white bread, crusts removed, cubed small
Breadcrumbs for coating
1 tablespoon vegetable oil
1 tablespoon butter

For the mustard sauce, in a small bowl stir together the mustard, chives and crème fraîche. Season to taste with salt and pepper. Set aside.

In a small mixing bowl, thoroughly mix the mayonnaise, egg, lemon juice, Worcestershire, Old Bay, salt and pepper. Set aside. Gently pick through the crabmeat and remove any shells. Toss the cubed bread with the crabmeat and gently fold in two-thirds of the mayonnaise mixture. If the crab can be formed into a ball without falling apart, it is ready; otherwise, add the remainder of the mayonnaise mixture. Divide and shape the crabmeat into 6 cakes. Heat the oil and butter in a skillet over medium heat. Coat the crab cakes with breadcrumbs and pan-fry until golden brown on both sides. Serve immediately topped with mustard sauce.

Serves 6

SOUTHERN-STYLE SHRIMP, SCALLOPS AND GRITS

Garlic Gravy
1 head garlic
½ cup red wine
1 sprig thyme
2 cups chicken stock
2 tablespoons flour
1 cup heavy cream
Kosher salt
Freshly ground black pepper

Grits
¾ cup water
½ cup milk
2 teaspoons butter
½ cup stone-ground grits
¼ cup heavy cream

8 large shrimp
2 large scallops
Olive oil
1 tablespoon chives, chopped

For the gravy, preheat oven to 350°. Cut the top of the garlic head off and season with salt and pepper. Wrap in foil and roast in oven for 40 minutes or until soft. Squeeze the roasted garlic from the peel. In a saucepan, heat the red wine with the thyme to a simmer. Stir in the garlic and simmer until reduced by two-thirds. Add the chicken stock and bring to a low boil. Mix the flour with 2 tablespoons water to form a paste. Whisk the flour mixture into the wine mixture, cook and reduce by one-third. Add the cream and return to a simmer. Strain and season to taste with salt and pepper.

In a saucepan, combine water with milk and butter and heat just to a boil. Stir in the grits and simmer on low heat 20-30 minutes or until the grits are soft. Stir frequently. If the mixture becomes too thick, add a little water. When the grits are cooked, stir in the cream and season to taste with salt and pepper.

Peel and devein the shrimp. Clean the scallops and trim off the tough "boot." Sauté in oil just until cooked, about 3 minutes. Add the garlic gravy to the pan and heat through. Serve in a bowl over the hot grits and garnish with chives.

Serves 4

LA TAVOLA TRATTORIA

CHEF JOEY MASI

In Italian, "la tavola" means "the table." In Atlanta, La Tavola means a cozy gathering place where friends can enjoy delicious, classic, yet updated, Italian cuisine in a comfortable setting. Consulting Chef Joey Masi helped create a menu that includes traditional pastas and sauces, as well as dishes that evoke the true taste of Italy's premier ingredients. Exposed brick, dark wood floors and rustic colors dominate in this neighborhood trattoria situated in the Virginia-Highland area.

BRUSCHETTA TOPPINGS

1 loaf day-old ciabatta or Italian bread
1 clove garlic, peeled

Olive Tapanade
½ pound Kalamata olives, chopped
4 ounces capers
1 bunch parsley, chopped
2 ounces olive oil
1 tablespoon chili flakes

Tuscan White Bean Salad
½ pound canned white beans
2 ounces carrots, minced
2 ounces onions, minced

2 ounces celery, minced
3 tablespoons olive oil
1 teaspoon salt
1 teaspoon pepper
1 bunch parsley, chopped

Tomato Salad
½ pound tomatoes, cut into small dice
1 large garlic clove, peeled and minced
3 tablespoons olive oil
½ bunch parsley, chopped
1 teaspoon salt
1 teaspoon pepper

For each topping, combine all ingredients and stir well. Cut bread into ½-inch slices. Toast or grill until light brown. Rub the top of each slice with a raw garlic clove. Spread the topping of your choice on each slice and serve.

Each Topping Serves 8 to 10

BOLOGNESE

2 tablespoons butter
3 tablespoons olive oil
6 ounces ground pork
6 ounces ground beef
6 ounces ground veal
6 ounces pancetta, cut into small dice
1 stalk of celery, diced
1 carrot, cut into small dice
1 onion, cut into small dice
½ cup red wine
1 cup chicken stock
1 pound tomatoes, peeled, seeded and diced
¼ cup heavy cream
3 tablespoons roughly chopped thyme
4 tablespoons chiffonade basil
Salt and pepper to taste

In a large saucepot, melt the butter with the oil. Add the ground pork, beef and veal. Cook thoroughly, then drain any fat left in the pot. Add the pancetta and cook. Add the celery, carrot and onion. Cook until soft. Add the wine and reduce by half. Add the chicken stock and tomatoes and bring to a simmer. When the liquid is reduced by half, (this may take up to an hour), add the cream, herbs and salt and pepper. Continue to cook about 5 more minutes or until sauce has a creamy consistency. Serve over pasta.

Serves 6 to 8

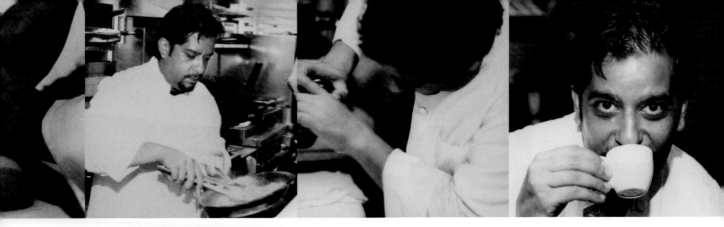

CAESAR DRESSING

2 egg yolks
2 cloves garlic, peeled
1½ ounces anchovies
1 tablespoon lemon juice
¼ cup distilled vinegar
1 tablespoon Dijon mustard
1½ ounces grated parmesan cheese
1¼ cups extra virgin olive oil
1 tablespoon pepper

In a food processor, combine all ingredients except olive oil and pepper. While processor is running, slowly incorporate the oil. Add pepper until blended. Serve over greens or refrigerate.

Makes 1 Pint

MUSSELS

12-15 large mussels
2 ounces tomato concasse
1 teaspoon fresh oregano
1 teaspoon fresh thyme
³/₄ cup dry vermouth
2 tablespoons butter
1 tablespoon flat-leaf parsley, chopped
Salt and pepper to taste

Rinse mussels well and clean by removing the beard. In a sauté pan, add the mussels, tomatoes, oregano, thyme and vermouth. Cover and bring to a simmer. When the mussels are open, season with salt and pepper. Add the butter and parsley. Stir until butter is melted. Serve immediately.

Serves 4

VEAL AND SPINACH MANICOTTI

Olive oil
1 medium yellow onion, diced
1 tablespoon garlic, chopped
1 pound ground veal
1 pound frozen chopped spinach, thawed
1 ¼ cups shredded mozzarella cheese, divided
Salt and pepper to taste
1 ½ cups tomato sauce
3 tablespoons grated parmesan cheese
3 tablespoons parsley, chopped
½ pound fresh pasta sheets or prepared manicotti shells

In a large saucepan, sauté onion and garlic in olive oil until translucent. Add ground veal and sauté until browned. Add chopped spinach and let cook for 10 minutes. Remove from heat and let cool. Add 1 cup mozzarella and mix thoroughly. Add salt and pepper to taste.

Preheat oven to 375°. Place a 4x3-inch fresh pasta sheet on a cutting board or table. Place 2-3 tablespoons of filling on pasta and roll into a tube. Place about half of the tomato sauce in the bottom of a baking dish. Arrange the manicotti in the dish on top of the sauce. Place another layer of tomato sauce on manicotti and sprinkle with remaining fresh mozzarella, grated parmesan and chopped parsley. Bake for 15-20 minutes.

Serves 4

THEO'S BROTHER'S BAKERY

BAKER YOLANDA ROJAS

Theo's Brother's Bakery in Alpharetta was inspired by the Old World bakeries of Europe. Offering an assortment of fresh breads, soups, sandwiches, baked goods and desserts, Theo's is the brainchild of chef/owners Michele and Christopher Sedgwick. Baker Yolanda Rojas begins baking early in the morning to ensure that patrons will find the perfect complement to any meal or occasion.

CHERRY FINANCIER

14 ounces unsalted butter
1 cup almonds, sliced
10⅜ ounces powdered sugar
3¼ ounces all-purpose flour
12 egg whites
1 teaspoon vanilla

2 tablespoons egg whites
2 tablespoons granulated sugar
¼ teaspoon cinnamon
1 cup almonds, sliced
30 fresh red cherries, pitted

In a heavy-bottomed saucepan, heat the butter until browned. Cool slightly. In the bowl of a food processor, grind the almonds, powdered sugar and flour to a fine powder, about 8 minutes. Gradually pulse in the egg whites, then the heated butter and vanilla. Be careful not to overprocess the mixture. Pour the mixture into a bowl and refrigerate for at least 4 hours or overnight.

In a small bowl, whisk egg whites until frothy. Add sugar, cinnamon and almonds and set aside.

When ready to bake, preheat convection oven to 375˚ (or conventional oven to 400˚). Grease 8 3-inch fluted pastry pans with removable bottoms. Fill pastry pans with cold financier batter just short of the top of the pan. Push 4 or 5 cherries into each pan. Generously top each pan with the almond topping. Bake until center is firm and cakes are golden brown, approximately 35 minutes. Remove cakes from pan immediately and let cool on wire rack.

Serves 8

BANANA NUT MUFFINS

4 ounces unsalted butter
1 cup sugar
2 eggs
6½ ounces all-purpose flour
1 teaspoon salt
1 teaspoon baking powder
1 teaspoon vanilla
4 bananas
½ cup sour cream
½ cup pecans, chopped
4 tablespoons raw sugar

Preheat oven to 350°. In a mixer fitted with a paddle, cream the butter and sugar together. Add eggs and beat until incorporated. Sift flour, salt and baking powder together and add to batter. In a food processor, purée bananas until smooth. Add bananas, sour cream, vanilla and nuts to the mixture and mix just until all ingredients are incorporated. Spray nonstick spray in muffin pans and fill with batter to the top of the muffin rim. Generously sprinkle raw sugar on top of each muffin. Bake until muffins are slightly puffed and lightly browned, approximately 25 minutes. Let cool in pan for 10 minutes and then remove to wire rack to finish cooling.

Makes 18 Muffins

PEYTON'S FAVORITE CHOCOLATE-ALMOND BISCOTTI

12 ounces all-purpose flour
1¼ cups sugar
½ cup cocoa
¾ teaspoon baking soda
1 tablespoon baking powder
¾ teaspoon salt
½ cup blanched, sliced almonds
¾ cup dried cranberries
6 tablespoons butter, melted
2 whole eggs
2 egg yolks
1 tablespoon vanilla
2 tablespoons orange zest

Preheat oven to 350°. Mix flour, sugar, cocoa, baking soda, baking powder, salt, almonds and cranberries in a large mixing bowl. In a medium-sized bowl, beat melted butter, eggs, egg yolks, vanilla and zest until combined, about 1 minute. Add to flour mixture and mix by hand until all ingredients are incorporated and a dough forms. Cut dough in half. On a greased and floured baking sheet, or on a parchment-lined baking sheet, pat dough into 2 logs, ½-inch thick x 1½ inches wide x 12 inches long. Place logs 2 inches apart. Bake for 40 minutes. Turn oven down to 250° and bake until almost hard but soft to the touch, about 10-15 minutes.

Remove from oven and cool on a wire rack for 45 minutes. With a serrated knife, cut loaves at a 45° angle into ½-inch-thick slices. Lay slices flat on baking sheet. Turn oven up to 275° and toast. Turn slices over and continue to toast until crisp. Cool on wire rack and store in airtight container.

Makes 32 Biscotti

RUSTIC RHUBARB BERRY TARTS

Pastry Dough

6 ounces unsalted butter, cut into 1-inch pieces
1 pound, 3 ounces all-purpose flour
1 tablespoon sugar
½ teaspoon salt
6 ounces cream cheese, cut into 1-inch pieces
¼ cup ice-cold water

Filling

4 cups rhubarb, cut in ½-inch pieces
2 cups blueberries

2 cups blackberries
¼ cup all-purpose flour
1 cup dark brown sugar
1 cup granulated sugar
1 teaspoon vanilla extract
1 teaspoon cinnamon
Zest from 1 orange

Topping

5 tablespoons butter, melted
1 cup raw sugar

For the pastry dough, combine butter, flour, sugar and salt in a mixer fitted with batter beater. Mix until a fine meal forms. Add the cream cheese and continue to mix until a fine meal forms again. Add ice water a little at a time and continue to mix just until a dough forms. Divide the dough into 2 equal discs. Cover with plastic wrap and refrigerate for at least 1 hour or overnight.

For the filling, toss the fruit in a large bowl with the flour, sugars, vanilla, cinnamon and orange zest until all ingredients are evenly mixed. Set aside.

Grease 6 3-inch fluted pastry rings with removable bottoms and set aside.

Remove 1 disk of pastry from refrigerator. Using a rolling pin, roll out the dough until it is approximately ⅛-inch thick. Cut the dough into 6-inch-diameter circles. Place the dough in one of the prepared pastry rings, being sure to gently press into the bottom and sides of rings. Allow the excess dough to drape over the lip of the tart pan. Spoon the filling in the tart pan, mounding it 1½ inches higher than the edge of the tart pan. Fold the excess dough over the filling, pinching and crimping it where necessary to cover the filling but leaving a small vent hole in the top. Reroll the scraps to make 2 more dough rounds. Continue with the second dough in the same manner.

Preheat convection oven to 375° (or conventional oven to 400°). Paint the top of the tarts with melted butter and generously sprinkle the raw sugar on top. Place the tarts on a baking sheet with sides, so as to avoid any spillovers in the oven. Bake tarts for 35 minutes, or until golden brown and the fruit is bubbling. Let cool on a wire rack before removing from tart pans.

Serves 6

SWEET POTATO BREAD WITH CORN AND JALAPEÑOS

1½ teaspoons active dry yeast
2 teaspoons barley malt syrup*
6 ounces water
¾ cup sweet potato, baked and peeled
½ cup yellow corn on the cob, grilled and cut off cob
1 jalapeño pepper, seeded and minced
9 ounces semolina flour
4½ ounces all-purpose flour
3 ounces cornmeal
1 tablespoon sea salt

Rehydrate yeast with barley malt syrup and water in a 1-cup glass measure. Combine all other ingredients except salt in a mixer fitted with batter beater. Mix on low speed and gradually add yeast mixture. Mix for 5 minutes. Allow dough to rest for 20 minutes. Add salt and mix on high speed for 5 minutes. Remove dough from mixer bowl and place on a cutting board covered with plastic wrap. Allow to proof for 1 hour.

Divide the dough into 2 pieces. Rub a little cornmeal on your hands and knead dough by gently rolling between your hands into a ball. Dough will be soft and slightly sticky but will hold together. Mist the dough with water and dust with additional cornmeal. Let dough rest for 1-2 hours, or until it springs back when pressed.

Preheat oven with baking stone to 400°. Cut a cross in top of dough to allow steam to escape while baking, or, for a more rustic bread, do not cut cross and allow dough to crack. Place dough on baking stone and mist with water. Mist the oven once and shut the door. Bake for 35 minutes. Test for doneness with an instant-reading thermometer, which should register 180° in the middle of the bread. Remove loaves from oven and cool on a wire rack.

* Barley malt syrup can be found at health food stores

Makes 2 loaves. Serves 8 to 10

HI LIFE
KITCHEN & COCKTAILS

CHEF CHRISTOPHER PYUN

With the finest in food, beverage and service, Hi Life kitchen & cocktails has come to be one of Atlanta's preferred restaurants. The innovative menu delights with American classics and an all-American wine list. Recipient of the coveted DiRōNA Award, the Norcross eatery guarantees an inimitable dining experience with its glowing atmosphere created by co-owner Tom DiGiorgio and the culinary talent of his co-owners, Chefs Christopher Pyun and John Metz.

BIG RAVIOLI

Ravioli
¼ cup olive oil
2 teaspoons garlic, minced
½ pound wild mushrooms, chopped
½ pound spinach, thoroughly rinsed and stemmed
½ pound feta cheese, crumbled
¼ cup mascarpone cheese
2 teaspoons Old Bay seasoning
¼ cup fresh basil leaves, thoroughly rinsed,
  stemmed and minced
Freshly ground black pepper
Kosher salt
6 fresh pasta sheets
1 egg

Sauce
2 tablespoons olive oil
½ cup onion, cut into small dice
4 cups heavy cream
2 tablespoons parsley, minced
2 tablespoons cilantro, minced
2 tablespoons chives, minced
1 tablespoon tarragon, minced
¼ teaspoon freshly ground black pepper
½ teaspoon salt

Herbs and feta cheese for garnish

MAINE LOBSTER AND WILD MUSHROOM SALAD

Fava Beans

¾ pound fresh or dried fava beans
2 quarts chicken stock
¼ cup carrots, cut into small dice
½ cup celery, cut into small dice
½ cup onion, cut into small dice
3 cloves garlic, crushed but left intact
1 sprig rosemary
1 sprig thyme
1 sprig basil

Salad

4 1½-2-pound live lobsters
1½ pounds assorted wild mushrooms (chanterelle, shiitake, cremini, morel, etc.)
2 bunches flat leaf spinach
1 bunch fresh arugula
Assorted sweet herbs such as basil, mint, tarragon
2 tablespoons extra virgin olive oil
1 tablespoon rice wine vinegar
1 tablespoon freshly squeezed lemon juice
Salt and pepper to taste

STUFFED VEAL WITH SHALLOTS, YUKON GOLD POTATOES AND ARUGULA

6 8-ounce veal loin medallions
8 ounces cremini mushrooms, sliced
8 ounces spinach, chopped
5 ounces olive oil, divided
¾ tablespoon chopped garlic, divided
8 ounces crawfish, tail meat
8 ounces asiago cheese, grated
12 medium Yukon gold potatoes, sliced
6 shallots, sliced
¼ tablespoon chopped garlic
¼ pound arugula, cleaned and chopped
Salt and pepper

Pound veal between plastic wrap until about ¼-inch thick. Set aside.

Sauté the mushrooms and spinach separately, each using 1 ounce of olive oil and ¼ tablespoon of the garlic, until tender and then chill.

Wash crawfish meat and dry. Squeeze any moisture from sautéed spinach and mushrooms. Combine crawfish, spinach, mushrooms and asiago cheese in a bowl and mix well.

On foil sheets large enough to hold each veal slice, drizzle 1 ounce olive oil, add salt and pepper and cover with veal slice. Put about ½ cup of stuffing mixture into veal, roll and wrap in foil.

Preheat oven to 450°. Unwrap veal and sauté in pan on each of its 4 sides for about 1 minute each. Then place in oven for 10–15 minutes.

Sauté potatoes, shallots and remaining garlic in 2 ounces olive oil until tender. Add arugula at last moment before serving. Season all well with salt and pepper.

Remove veal from oven, let set about 5 minutes. Slice and serve with potato mixture.

Serves 6

SWEET AUBURN BREAD COMPANY

CHEF SONYA JONES

Once inside the historic Sweet Auburn Curb Market in downtown Atlanta, the aroma of baked breads and sweets will lead you straight to Sonya Jones. The owner and chef of Sweet Auburn Bread Company, Jones puts smiles on the faces of customers seeking to indulge their sweet tooth. She loves to use regional items in her fresh-from-the-oven sweet breads, pies, layer cakes and homemade cookies. Honored with a visit from President Bill Clinton in 1999, Sweet Auburn Bread Company's sweet potato cheesecake received the presidential "seal of approval."

CAST-IRON SKILLET CORNBREAD

3 tablespoons vegetable shortening or bacon grease
2 cups cornmeal
2 teaspoons baking powder
2 tablespoons sugar
2 teaspoons salt
2 cups buttermilk
2 eggs, beaten
2 tablespoons melted butter

Preheat oven to 425°. Coat a 9-inch cast-iron skillet with the shortening/grease and place in heated oven. Combine cornmeal, baking powder, sugar and salt in a mixing bowl. Stir in the buttermilk, eggs and melted butter until just combined. Pour into hot cast-iron skillet. Bake for 25 minutes.

Serves 8

SWEET POTATO PIE

Pastry Dough
1¼ cups flour
½ teaspoon salt
3 ounces butter or shortening
¼ cup cold water

Filling
2 cups sweet potatoes, peeled, diced and cooked
1 cup sugar
1 teaspoon fresh nutmeg, grated
3 eggs
1½ cups half and half
½ cup melted butter
¼ teaspoon pure vanilla extract
¼ teaspoon pure lemon extract

For dough, combine flour and salt and cut in shortening with pastry blender until mixture is the texture of cornmeal. Add cold water, mix until moistened and shape into a ball and press flat. Wrap in plastic and chill.

Preheat oven to 350˚. Roll dough to ½-inch thick on a lightly floured surface. Place in a 9-inch pie plate and trim any excess edges.

For filling, mix sweet potatoes in a bowl, add sugar and nutmeg and mix well. Add eggs, one at a time, and mix well. Add half and half and mix well. Add butter and flavors. Pour into prepared pastry shell. Bake for 45–50 minutes.

Serves 6 to 8

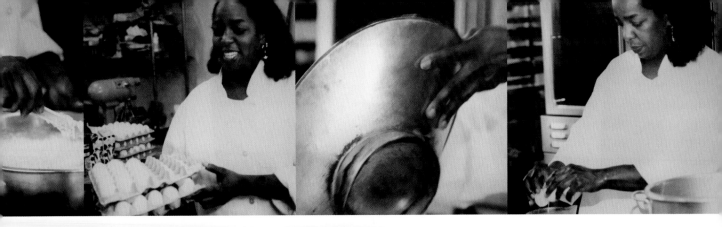

BUTTERED YEAST ROLLS

1 package active dry yeast (1 scant tablespoon)
1 cup warm water
1 tablespoon sugar
2 teaspoons shortening
½ teaspoon salt
3 cups bread flour
2 tablespoons butter, melted

Dissolve yeast in warm (110°) water. Stir gently and let rest for 2 minutes to proof. In the bowl of a mixer fitted with a dough hook, add the proofed yeast, sugar, shortening, salt and flour. Mix on low speed 1 minute. Turn speed up and mix for 5-8 minutes until the dough forms one ball and is smooth and silky. Turn onto a floured surface and knead for 1 minute. Grease the top of the dough with 1 tablespoon of melted butter, cover and let rise in a warm place until double in bulk, about 1 hour.

Preheat oven to 425°. Punch dough down, turn onto a lightly floured surface and knead 8-10 times. Roll the dough into a long cylinder and cut into 12 even pieces. Place on greased sheet pan and bake for 20 minutes or until golden brown. Remove from the oven and brush with the other tablespoon of melted butter.

Serves 6

LEMON BUTTERMILK CHESS PIE

2 cups sugar
1 tablespoon flour
1 tablespoon cornmeal
¼ teaspoon salt
1 tablespoon lemon zest, grated
¼ cup freshly squeezed lemon juice
¼ cup buttermilk
4 eggs, beaten
¼ cup butter, melted
1 unbaked 9-inch pastry shell

Preheat oven to 350°. In a large mixing bowl, combine sugar, flour, cornmeal and salt. Add lemon zest, lemon juice and buttermilk. Whisk mixture until ingredients are mixed. Add beaten eggs and melted butter and continue to whisk ingredients until well combined. Pour into unbaked pastry shell and bake for 45 minutes, or until top of pie is lightly browned. The filling will firm up as pie cools. Cool to room temperature, then refrigerate until serving time.

Serves 8

OLD-FASHIONED POUND CAKE WITH BRANDIED APRICOT GLAZE

Cake
Oil
Flour
1 pound butter
3 cups sugar
6 eggs
20 ounces (4 cups) all-purpose flour
1 cup half and half
1 tablespoon pure vanilla extract
1 tablespoon pure lemon extract

Brandied Apricot Glaze
10 ounces apricot preserves
1 teaspoon ginger, freshly grated
3 ounces brandy

For the cake, spray a 10-inch tube pan and dust lightly with flour. Set aside.

Cream the butter and sugar in a mixer with the batter beater on medium speed. Add eggs one at a time, beating well after each addition. Scrape the sides of the bowl often. Change mixer speed to low and alternately add flour and half and half, starting and ending with flour. Add vanilla and lemon extracts. Scrape the bowl again to ensure even blending and spoon batter into prepared 10-inch tube pan. Give pan a sharp rap on counter to dislodge any air bubbles. Place cake in a COLD oven and set to 350°. Bake for 1 hour 35 minutes or until tester comes out clean. Cake will rise slightly above pan and top may crack slightly. Remove cake from oven and let cool in pan for 15 minutes. Remove from pan and continue to cool on wire rack.

For the glaze, heat apricot preserves and stir until melted. Add ginger and let mixture cool slightly. Add brandy and cool to room temperature. Pour glaze over warm cake and let it drip down sides.

Serves 12

BOLD AMERICAN FOOD COMPANY

CHEF KURT D'AURIZIO

Tastefully innovative, Bold American Food Company provides restaurant-quality food at Atlanta's best social and business events. Chef Kurt D'Aurizio and his staff present fully customized menus drawing upon fine American, European and Asian cuisine with contemporary twists. The food is prepared from scratch and includes home-baked breads, pastries and desserts.

CITRUS-MARINATED BLACKENED SHRIMP AND TANGERINE

2 cups freshly squeezed orange juice
1 cup freshly squeezed lime juice
1 cup water
½ cup salt
1½ teaspoons black peppercorns
1½ teaspoons coriander

½ teaspoon brown sugar
25 medium 16–20 count shrimp, peeled and deveined
1 cup Cajun spice
25 tangerines, in wedges
25 sugarcane skewers, 4–6 inches long

Make a brine with the orange juice, lime juice, water, salt, black peppercorns, coriander and brown sugar. Heat the brine to dissolve the salt and sugar, then chill. Add shrimp and let it sit in the brine for 1 hour. Remove shrimp from the brine, rinse well and pat dry. Coat shrimp in Cajun spice and skewer along with the tangerine wedges on the sugarcane skewers. Grill for approximately 2 minutes on each side.

Serves 6

CHILLED CUCUMBER SOUP WITH CRÈME FRAÎCHE

Cucumber Soup

3 cucumbers, washed, seeded, half peeled, half not
1 tablespoon ginger, peeled and diced
1 tablespoon shallots, peeled and diced
1 ½ tablespoons freshly squeezed lime juice
Sea salt and white pepper to taste

Crème Fraîche

2 cups crème fraîche (may substitute sour cream or heavy cream whipped into soft peaks)
1 tablespoon honey
1 tablespoon freshly squeezed lime juice
Sea salt and white pepper to taste

Garnish

1 tablespoon mint, chiffonade
1 tablespoon cilantro, chiffonade
1 tablespoon red pepper, brunoise

For the soup, purée all ingredients, taste for seasoning and adjust as necessary. Pass through a fine mesh strainer. Set aside.

For the crème fraîche, mix all ingredients together and blend well. Set aside.

In a small bowl combine all garnish ingredients.

To serve, ladle approximately 6 fluid ounces of cucumber soup into each bowl. Top with a teaspoon of crème fraîche and garnish with a pinch of the garnish combination.

Serves 6

PONZU-MARINATED BEEF SATAY

Beef Satay
1 pound beef flank steak
4-inch skewers

Ponzu Sauce
1 cup soy sauce
½ cup sherry
2 teaspoons garlic, chopped
2 teaspoons ginger, peeled and chopped
½ lemon, zest and juice
½ lime, zest and juice
½ orange, zest and juice
½ teaspoon chili flakes
½ teaspoon fresh cilantro
2 tablespoons sesame oil
1 teaspoon sugar

Slice beef thin and skewer on 4-inch skewers. Set aside. In a separate bowl, combine all ingredients for Ponzu sauce. Reserve ½ cup. Marinate beef skewers in Ponzu sauce overnight.

Brush skewers with Ponzu sauce. Grill to your liking. Brush skewers with reserved Ponzu sauce and serve.

Serves 4 to 6

VIETNAMESE LETTUCE WRAPS

Filling
1 pound ground chicken breast
2 tablespoons sesame oil
1 tablespoon fresh ginger, peeled and chopped
1 tablespoon fresh garlic, chopped
1 carrot, julienned
10 snow peas, julienned
2 scallions, chopped
2 tablespoons sweet soy sauce
1 tablespoon sriracha
¼ cup cashews

Lettuce Wraps
2 heads red-leaf Bibb lettuce
1 pint alfalfa, radish or mixed sprouts

In a sauté pan, sear chicken breast in sesame oil. Once chicken is golden brown, add all of the ingredients except the cashews. Stir in the sweet soy sauce and sriracha. Add cashews.

Clean lettuce. Remove leaves whole from each head.

Place chicken mixture in each bowl. Place whole lettuce leaves around mixture. Garnish with sprouts.

Serves 8 to 10

SAVORY CORNBREAD PUDDING

1 loaf cornbread (or 1 dozen corn muffins)
1 tablespoon butter
1 red bell pepper, diced small
1 ear corn, roasted in husk on grill
½ jalapeño pepper, diced small
1 bunch green onions, thinly sliced
1 quart cream
4 eggs
4 egg yolks
Salt and pepper to taste
¼ teaspoon cayenne pepper

Cut cornbread into large dice and bake on a sheet pan until crispy (similar to a crouton). Melt butter in a sauté pan and add all vegetables except onions. Let simmer for 5 minutes. Remove from heat and stir in green onions. In a separate bowl, beat together cream, eggs and egg yolks. Season with salt and pepper.

Preheat oven to 350˚. Place cornbread croutons into buttered serving dish. Add sautéed peppers, onions and corn. Pour egg mixture over vegetables to about 1-1½ inches from the edge of dish.

Bake until golden brown on top and the custard is set.

Serves 8 to 10

FISHBONE RESTAURANT
AND THE PIRANHA BAR

CHEF RICHARD BLAIS

Fishbone Restaurant and The Piranha Bar has fulfilled its promise to provide the freshest, most delicious seafood in the most comfortable, entertaining setting this side of the coast. Chef Richard Blais has been associated with some of the top seafood restaurants in the U.S. and now sets the course at this beloved restaurant docked in Buckhead.

BARELY COOKED ORGANIC MAINE SALMON

Pickling Liquid
1 cup water
½ cup rice wine vinegar
½ cup sugar
1 tablespoon red pepper flakes
2 tablespoons black pepper

1 cucumber, thinly sliced
4 radishes, thinly sliced
1 carrot, thinly sliced
½ red onion, thinly sliced

Yogurt Sauce
1 cup Old Chatham Yogurt (or unsweetened plain yogurt)
¼ cup diced cucumber
4 tablespoons dill
Salt and pepper
1 lemon, freshly squeezed

4 6-ounce salmon fillets

For the pickling liquid, combine all ingredients in a small saucepan, bring to a boil and then chill. Combine liquid with the sliced vegetables and reserve.

For the yogurt sauce, combine yogurt with diced cucumber, dill, salt, pepper and lemon juice. For a variation add cumin and mint.

Season salmon fillets with salt and pepper and cook skin-side down over low heat, preferably in a nonstick pan. Cook for approximately 2 minutes on each side. If you do not like raw or barely cooked fish, cook salmon on medium flame for 4 minutes on each side. Plate salmon over pickled vegetables and sauce with yogurt.

Serves 4

OAK-GRILLED TUNA "FILET MIGNON"
WITH PARSNIP PURÉE AND RED WINE SHALLOTS

Purée
2 pounds parsnips
1 pound potatoes
1 cup heavy cream
1 pound butter
Salt and white pepper to taste

Sauce
1 bottle red wine (red zinfandel)
1 cup shallots, chopped
1 tablespoon butter
1 tablespoon allspice

4 8-ounce pieces of tuna

Peel parsnips and potatoes and place in a large pot of boiling, salted water. Cook until tender. Drain potatoes and parsnips. Warm heavy cream over medium heat in a saucepan. Mix or crush potatoes and parsnips with heated cream and fold in cold butter. (This all needs to be done hot.) Season with salt and pepper and set aside.

For the red wine sauce, reduce the bottle of red zinfandel in a saucepan with the chopped shallots until ½ cup remains. Cook reduction for 5 minutes and, while sauce is warm, whisk in butter, slowly. Add allspice. Set aside.

Season tuna with salt and pepper. Grill until medium rare, approximately 5 minutes on each side. Plate tuna over parsnip purée. Pour red wine sauce over tuna and serve immediately.

Serves 4

RED SNAPPER WITH SUMMER VEGETABLES

4 6-ounce snapper fillets
12 cherry tomatoes, halved
1 zucchini, julienned
1 red onion, julienned
2 tablespoons garlic, minced
2 tablespoons fresh basil
2 tablespoons fresh oregano
2 tablespoons fresh parsley
4 ounces dry white wine
4 ounces extra virgin olive oil
Salt and pepper to taste
1 lemon, sliced

Preheat oven to 400°. Season fish with salt and pepper. Place all ingredients in a Pyrex casserole, making sure there are veggies under and on top of fish. Lather everything with the oil and salt and pepper, and top with lemon slices. Cover with aluminum foil, making sure no air can penetrate casserole. Bake for approximately 13 minutes, or until fish has turned opaque.

Serves 4

ROASTED CASCO BAY COD LOIN
WITH BRAISED CABBAGE AND CHORIZO

1 large onion, thinly sliced
1 large carrot, chopped into large dice
4 links chorizo, halved
½ pound butter, divided
1 head cabbage, shredded
1 sachet of thyme, parsley, bay leaf, garlic & cloves
1 cup chicken stock
1 russet potato, shredded
1 Granny Smith apple, julienned
¼ cup champagne vinegar
4 tablespoons Pommery mustard
Salt and pepper to taste
4 6-ounce Casco Bay cod fillets
Thyme and smashed garlic for seasoning

Preheat oven to 400°. In a heavy-bottomed saucepan, sauté onion, carrot and chorizo in 1 tablespoon butter. Cook for 20 minutes. Add cabbage and sachet of herbs. Cook for 5 minutes.

Add stock, shredded potato and apple into cabbage mix. Cook until everything is tender. Finish with vinegar, mustard, salt, pepper and 7 tablespoons butter. Reserve warm.

Salt and pepper cod fillets and place on a baking sheet with 8 tablespoons butter, thyme and smashed garlic. Bake for 7 minutes. Serve with cabbage mixture on the side.

Serves 4

SOFT-SHELL CRAB "SANDWICH" WITH BABY SPINACH SALAD
AND BACON VINAIGRETTE

1 tablespoon curry powder
½ cup mayonnaise
1 tablespoon honey
8 slices toasted brioche
¼ pound applewood smoked bacon, diced
2 tablespoons sherry vinegar
½ red onion, sliced thin
1 pound arrowleaf spinach, washed and drained
Salt and pepper
½ cup flour
4 jumbo soft-shell crabs
2 lemons, halved

Combine curry powder, mayonnaise and honey to make a curry mayonnaise. Spread on brioche and set aside.

For the salad, render bacon until crispy. Remove bacon from pan and add sherry vinegar and onion to the bacon fat. Drizzle this vinaigrette over the spinach while hot, wilting the leaves. Garnish with bacon pieces.

For the crab, season with salt and pepper. Dust with flour and sauté in a hot oiled pan for approximately 2 minutes on each side. Drain off oil. Place between 2 pieces of prepared brioche. Serve with a squeeze of lemon juice on each crab and the salad on the side.

Serves 4

ARIA

PASTRY CHEF KATHRYN KING

At Aria, Pastry Chef Kathryn King prepares delectable desserts using the season's freshest ingredients. Her creations perfectly complement the flavors of Aria's slow-cooked American cuisine, and make this restaurant a favorite amongst the serious food crowd. King delights diners with her virtuosity on sweet finishes.

VANILLA-ROASTED PLUMS WITH TOASTED LEMON POUND CAKE

14 tablespoons unsalted butter, divided	$\frac{1}{2}$ teaspoon salt
3 $\frac{1}{4}$ cups sugar, divided	$\frac{3}{4}$ cup buttermilk
5 eggs, separated	
2 lemons, zest and juice	9 black plums
3 cups cake flour	1 vanilla bean
$\frac{1}{2}$ teaspoon baking soda	Ice cream

For the cake, preheat oven to 350°. Prepare a 10" tube pan by lightly greasing and dusting with sugar. In a mixer, cream 12 tablespoons butter and 2 cups sugar until light and fluffy. Scrape sides of bowl and mix until all combined. Add egg yolks, scraping down the sides of the bowl and mixing thoroughly. Add 2½ tablespoons lemon juice and the zest of both lemons. Sift the flour, baking soda and salt together in a separate bowl. Alternately add to the creamed mixture with the buttermilk, ending with the milk. Whip the egg whites with ¼ cup sugar until soft peaks form. Gently fold the egg whites into the cake batter. Pour the batter into the prepared tube pan. Bake for about 1 hour, or until a toothpick comes out clean. Cool slightly in pan, then turn out onto parchment paper to fully cool.

For the plums, preheat oven to 325°. Split the plums and remove seeds. Place cut-side up in a baking dish. Split the vanilla bean, scrape the seeds out and mix with the remaining cup of sugar. Sprinkle over the plums and put the vanilla pod in the baking dish. Bake until the plums are very soft, about 45 minutes to 1 hour, depending on the variety and ripeness of the plums. Remove the fruit and reduce the liquid in a saucepan until it is syrupy, about 15 minutes. The peels will naturally slip off the plums. Remove the peels from the cooling plums. Stir the roasted plums into the sauce, set aside and keep warm.

In a heavy sauté pan, melt the 2 remaining tablespoons butter. Slice the cake and toast each slice in the sauté pan until lightly browned on both sides. Place a toasted cake slice on each plate and spoon some of the plums and sauce over. Just before serving, add a scoop of your favorite ice cream.

Serves 12

CARAMELIZED CHOCOLATE TRUFFLES

2 tablespoons sugar
Water
¼ cup heavy cream
1 tablespoon unsalted butter
½ pound best-quality dark/bittersweet chocolate, chopped
4 ounces of your favorite nuts (pecans, hazelnuts, pistachios, etc.)

In a small, heavy-bottomed saucepan, measure the sugar and add just enough water to cover, no more than 2 tablespoons. Bring to a boil over high heat and cook until the sugar begins to caramelize and turn a deep brown color, about 3-4 minutes. Remove from the heat. In a separate bowl or pan, warm the cream and carefully, pouring away from you, add to the hot sugar mixture. When the bubbling subsides, whisk together and then whisk in the butter and chocolate and stir until melted. Pour into a small loaf pan and cool to room temperature.

Toast the nuts just until fragrant and grind very fine. When the chocolate has set and solidified, scoop into bite-sized pieces with a melon baller or small scoop onto a plate and chill. Working quickly, reroll each ball and dredge in toasted, ground nuts. Keep at room temperature. These may be kept in an airtight container in a cool place for up to 1 week.

Makes about 2 dozen truffles

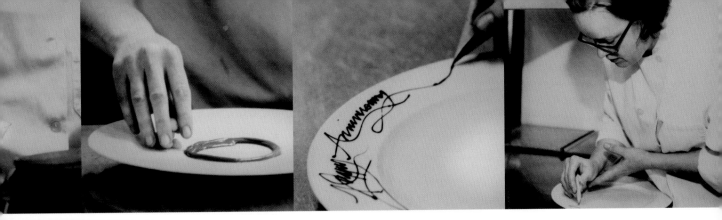

PANNA COTTA WITH TANGERINES

3½ teaspoons gelatin powder, divided
9 tangerines, divided
1¾ cups heavy cream
½ vanilla bean
1 cup sugar, divided
1 cup sour cream
½ cup water

For the panna cotta, sprinkle 2½ teaspoons gelatin over the juice of 2 tangerines to soften. In a small saucepan, heat the heavy cream, split the vanilla bean and scrape the seeds, adding to the cream along with the bean. Add the zest of 2 tangerines and 6 tablespoons sugar to the cream and bring just to a simmer. Remove from the heat. Add the softened gelatin and stir to dissolve. Remove from the heat and strain through a fine sieve. Whisk in the sour cream. Divide evenly into 4 ramekins and chill until set.

For the candied tangerine peel, remove the zest of 6 tangerines, being careful to avoid the white, bitter pith. Cut in long, thin strips. Juice the 6 tangerines and reserve ½ cup for the topping. Set aside. In a small saucepan, cover the zest with water and bring to a boil. Strain and repeat this process two more times. After straining the third time, add ½ cup sugar and ½ cup water to the pan and simmer with the peel until zest is tender, about 15 minutes. Remove from heat and let cool in syrup. When cool, remove to a cooling rack and sprinkle with 1 tablespoon sugar.

For the topping, mix the remaining 1 teaspoon gelatin with remaining 1 tablespoon sugar. Sprinkle over ¼ cup of the tangerine juice to soften. In a small saucepan, gently warm the remaining ¼ cup tangerine juice. Mix in the softened gelatin and stir until dissolved. Pour over the chilled panna cotta and allow to set.

Section the remaining tangerine and place on top of the chilled panna cotta. Garnish with the candied tangerine peel. This is a light and refreshing custard.

Serves 4

SOUR CREAM CAKE WITH CARAMEL NUT SAUCE

Cake
16 tablespoons (2 sticks) unsalted butter
2 cups sugar
4 eggs
3¼ cups flour
4 teaspoons baking powder
2 teaspoons salt
2 teaspoons vanilla extract
2 cups sour cream

Caramel Nut Sauce
2 cups sugar
1 teaspoon lemon juice
2 cups heavy cream
8 tablespoons unsalted butter
1 cup assorted nuts, toasted

Preheat oven to 350°. Butter a 10-inch cake pan and dust with flour. In the bowl of an electric mixer with a paddle attachment, cream the butter until light and fluffy. Slowly add the sugar and beat until light and fluffy, scraping the sides, and paddle down frequently. Add the eggs one at a time, mixing after each addition until incorporated. Sift the dry ingredients together in a separate bowl. Alternately add the dry ingredients and the vanilla and sour cream to the creamed mixture mixing just until incorporated. Put the batter into the prepared pan. Bake until the center, when pressed lightly, springs back, about 1 hour or more. Cool completely in pan and turn out onto a serving platter.

For the sauce, in a large, heavy-bottomed stainless or copper saucepan, heat the sugar and just enough water to moisten. Add the lemon juice. Boil over medium-high heat, cleaning the sides of the pan with a pastry brush dipped in water to make sure the mixture does not crystallize. When the sugar mixture begins to turn light brown, remove from the heat and carefully stir in the heavy cream. When the bubbling has stopped, whisk in the butter. Add the toasted nuts and keep warm until serving.

Pour the warm sauce over the warm cake. Slice and serve with ice cream.

Serves 8

WARM CHOCOLATE CHEESECAKE

Crust

1½ cups finely ground pecans
¼ cup sugar
8 tablespoons unsalted butter, melted

Filling

4 ounces dark/bittersweet chocolate
24 ounces cream cheese
¾ cup sugar
3 eggs

For the crust, preheat oven to 350°. Mix the pecans and sugar in a medium bowl. Add just enough melted butter to allow the mixture to hold together when pressed in your palm. Spread evenly into a buttered 10" springform pan and press down. Bake until browned, about 10-12 minutes. Remove from the oven and set aside to cool. Turn oven down to 300°.

In a double boiler, melt the chocolate and set aside to cool. In the bowl of an electric mixer fitted with the paddle, beat the cream cheese until smooth, scraping the sides of the bowl and the beater and beating again until smooth. Add the sugar and mix again until smooth. Add the eggs one at a time, beating until smooth. Again, scrape the sides of the bowl and the beater and mix all until smooth. Remove 1 cup of the batter and fold into the melted chocolate. Pour the remaining batter into the prepared crust. Slowly, in a spiral motion, pour the chocolate mixture onto the cream cheese mixture. Using a fork, gently swirl the chocolate into the cream cheese mixture. Bake just until the cake puffs around the edges and begins to set in the center, about 1 hour. Remove from the oven and let cool in the pan.

The batter may be made the day before and stored in the refrigerator. The wonderful texture of the cake is dependent on its never being chilled, so it is best baked just before or a few hours before serving. It is delicious served with some lightly sweetened soft whipped cream and chocolate sauce.

Serves 8

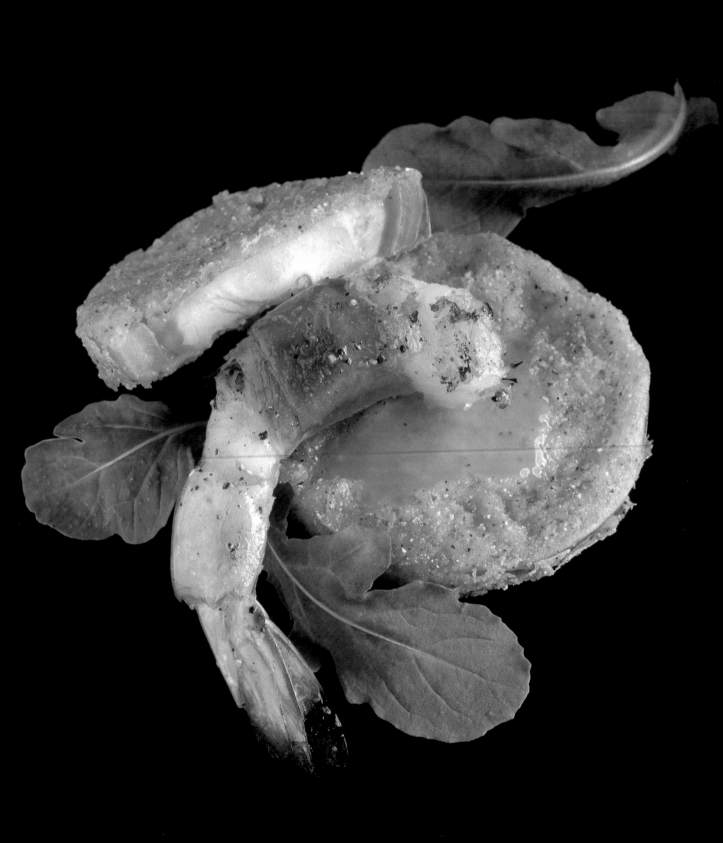

1848 HOUSE

CHEF TOM MCEACHERN

A family-owned and -operated residence-turned-restaurant, 1848 House offers both Southern elegance and cutting-edge cuisine. This Greek Revival plantation home in Marietta is listed on the National Historic Registry and features 11 dining rooms, each decorated with authentic furnishings of the 1840s and 1850s. Invited to cook at the James Beard House in New York in 1999, Chef Tom McEachern delights patrons with his acclaimed contemporary Southern cuisine.

GRILLED SHRIMP WRAPPED IN PROSCIUTTO WITH FRIED GREEN TOMATOES AND PASSION FRUIT VINAIGRETTE

Vinaigrette
¼ cup passion fruit purée (soak dried passion fruit
    until soft and purée in blender)
¼ cup sugar
⅓ cup rice wine vinegar
Pinch of salt
1¼ shallots, minced
1½ cups extra virgin olive oil

Fried Green Tomatoes
1 cup buttermilk
1 egg
3 tablespoons Cajun seasoning, divided
¼ teaspoon cayenne pepper
Salt and pepper
1 cup yellow cornmeal
1 cup all-purpose flour
1 tablespoon dried oregano
3 green tomatoes
4 tablespoons vegetable oil

Shrimp
1 pound large shrimp, 16-20 per pound
¼ pound thinly sliced prosciutto
1 bunch basil
12 wooden skewers

4 cups arugula

Combine all the vinaigrette ingredients except the oil in a small saucepan. Bring to a boil and stir to dissolve the sugar, then remove from the heat. Let cool slightly. Emulsify the mixture by whisking and slowly adding the oil. Set aside.

For the fried green tomatoes, whisk the buttermilk, egg, 1 tablespoon of Cajun seasoning, cayenne pepper, salt and pepper together in a medium-sized bowl and chill. Meanwhile, mix cornmeal, all-purpose flour, oregano and 2 tablespoons of Cajun seasoning in another medium-sized bowl. Core the green tomatoes and slice ¼-inch thick. Place tomato slices in buttermilk mixture and let macerate for a few minutes. Remove tomato slices from buttermilk mixture and dredge in flour mixture. Heat fry pan and when it is hot, add oil. Add as many tomato slices as the pan will allow without crowding. Sauté the tomato slices on both sides until golden brown. Drain on paper towels. Half tomato slices.

Peel and devein the shrimp, leaving the tail intact. Roll the basil leaves and prosciutto around each shrimp. Place three shrimp on each double skewer. Grill the shrimp on a preheated grill until shrimp turn white near the inside.

Toss the arugula with just enough passion fruit vinaigrette to flavor it and place in the center of a large plate. Remove the shrimp from the skewers and place around the tossed arugula. Place the fried green tomato halves between the shrimp to alternate them. Serve immediately. If you have any leftover fried green tomato halves, they are for the cook!

Serves 6

1848 CHARLESTON SHE CRAB SOUP

5 tablespoons butter, divided
1 small onion, finely chopped
1 bay leaf
¼ teaspoon dried tarragon
¼ teaspoon dried thyme
2 ounces all-purpose flour
1 quart cold fish stock or low sodium clam juice
1 cup heavy cream
¼ cup dry sherry or Madeira wine
8 ounces lump crabmeat
2 ounces crab roe
Kosher salt and cayenne pepper to taste
Paprika

In a heavy-bottomed 8-quart saucepan, combine 4 tablespoons butter, onion, bay leaf, tarragon and thyme and sauté on medium heat until tender. Do not allow onion to brown. Add flour and stir until mixture turns opaque and ingredients are well combined. Add cold fish stock or clam juice and bring to a boil, stirring frequently. Reduce heat and simmer soup until thickened and taste of raw flour has disappeared. Add heavy cream, sherry, crabmeat and roe. Season to taste with salt and cayenne pepper. Swirl in remaining butter just before serving. Garnish with additional crabmeat and sprinkling of paprika.

Serves 8

VENISON STEAKS ON VEGETABLE CHILI WITH FRIED ONIONS
AND SOUR CREAM

Vegetable Chili

3 ounces black-eyed peas
3 ounces baby lima beans
3 ounces red kidney beans
3 ounces black beans
3 tablespoons chili powder
2 teaspoons ground cumin
2 teaspoons paprika
2 teaspoons dried oregano
½ teaspoon cayenne pepper
2 tablespoons extra virgin olive oil
1 medium red onion, diced
½ green pepper, seeded and diced
½ red pepper, seeded and diced
½ yellow pepper, seeded and diced
1 small jalapeño pepper, seeded and diced
1 clove garlic, minced
½ cup red wine
2 medium tomatoes, cored and diced
1 16-ounce can whole tomatoes, drained and cut up
1 cup chicken stock
Corn from one ear of grilled corn
Salt

Fried Onions

2 yellow onions
¼ cup flour
½ teaspoon cayenne pepper
3 tablespoons vegetable oil
Sour cream

Venison Steaks

6 venison steaks, 4-5 ounces each
3 tablespoons olive oil
Sea salt and freshly ground pepper

For the vegetable chili, pour the peas and beans in a colander and rinse, removing any small stones. Soak each type of bean separately. Rinse the beans again and cook each type of bean separately. The black-eyed peas will take approximately 20 minutes to cook; the other beans will take about 30 minutes. Drain the beans and set aside. Heat a dry skillet over medium heat and toast the chili powder, cayenne pepper, paprika, ground cumin, and dried oregano until they become fragrant. Be careful not to let them burn. Heat oil in a large sauté pan. Add onions, peppers, garlic and jalapeño pepper and cook over medium heat until they are soft and translucent, about 5 minutes. Add the toasted spices. Add wine and cook until pan is almost dry. Stir frequently to prevent burning. Add tomatoes, canned and fresh, beans and corn. Add chicken stock and simmer until liquid is reduced by two-thirds, approximately 20 minutes. Season with salt to taste.

For the fried onions and garnish, slice the onions very thin. Stir together the cayenne and flour. Dredge the onions in this mixture and fry in oil until golden brown. Season with salt and pepper and reserve. Slightly whip sour cream until smooth. Place in a plastic squeeze bottle.

For the venison steaks, heat cast-iron skillet until hot. Add oil and steaks and cook steaks to medium rare, about 2 minutes per side. Remove from skillet and season with sea salt and freshly ground pepper.

Assemble plate by putting a mound of vegetable chili on plate. Put cooked venison steak on top of chili and garnish with onions. Squeeze design of sour cream over onions. Serve immediately.

Serves 6 to 8

SAUTÉED SEA SCALLOPS WITH SPECKLED WHITE CHEDDAR GRITS AND GOLDEN PINEAPPLE-SAGE BUTTER

Pineapple-Sage Butter
3 shallots, chopped
½ cup golden pineapple, cored and diced fine
3 tablespoons pineapple sage, divided
3 green peppercorns
1 bay leaf
1 cup white wine
¼ cup heavy cream
¼ cup unsalted butter
Salt and pepper to taste

Cheddar Cheese Grits
1 cup half and half
½ cup stone-ground grits
1½ cups chicken stock
3 ounces sharp white cheddar cheese, grated
Salt and pepper to taste

Scallops
12 large scallops
2 tablespoons extra virgin olive oil
Pepper to taste

For pineapple-sage butter, place the shallots, half the pineapple, half the pineapple sage, peppercorns and bay leaf with the white wine in a 2-quart pot. Reduce mixture until almost dry. Add heavy cream and reduce mixture for 2 minutes. Whisk in the butter, one tablespoon at a time, over medium-high heat. Strain through a fine strainer. Add the remaining pineapple sage and pineapple. Season with salt and pepper. Keep mixture warm and set aside.

For the grits, bring the half and half to a boil. Add the grits and reduce heat. Simmer until thick, stirring constantly. Add chicken stock ¼ cup at a time. Just before serving, add cheddar cheese and stir. Season with salt and pepper and set aside. Add more stock if necessary.

For the scallops, heat a small sauté pan over medium-high heat. Add the olive oil. Season scallops with black pepper and sauté until there is a warm center, about 2 minutes per side. Remove from pan and set aside.

Place a spoonful of grits in the center of each plate. Place a scallop on top of the grits. Sauce the scallop with the pineapple sage butter. Serve immediately.

Serves 4 to 6

TUNA TARTARE

¼ cup soy sauce
3 tablespoons mirin
1 tablespoon sake
¼ cup sesame oil
1 tablespoon + 1 teaspoon extra virgin olive oil
1 teaspoon ginger, peeled and minced
1 teaspoon garlic, minced
½ teaspoon cayenne pepper
½ teaspoon freshly ground black pepper
1½ pounds sushi-grade tuna, chilled
⅓ cup pine nuts
2½ tablespoons sesame seeds
½ Golden Delicious apple, peeled
¼ European cucumber, peeled and seeded
3 scallions, white and tender green

In a small nonreactive saucepan, bring soy sauce, mirin and sake to a boil over high heat. Cook until reduced to ⅓ cup, about 4 minutes. Transfer to a bowl and cool completely. Add sesame oil and 1 tablespoon olive oil, ginger, garlic, cayenne pepper and black pepper. Allow mixture to stand at room temperature for at least 2 hours or overnight.

Using a sharp knife, slice the tuna into small dice, working quickly to keep the tuna as cold as possible. Transfer diced tuna to a bowl and keep chilled.

Heat the remaining teaspoon of olive oil in a small skillet and add pine nuts and lightly toast, about 4 minutes. Remove pine nuts to a paper towel to blot excess oil and let cool. Meanwhile in the same skillet, toast sesame seeds until golden, about 2 minutes. Coarsely chop toasted pine nuts, mix with toasted sesame seeds and set aside. Dice apple, cucumber and scallions and set aside.

Just before serving, combine in a bowl the chilled tuna, toasted pine nuts and sesame seeds, apple, cucumber and scallions. Whisk the sauce and add ½ cup of the sauce to tuna mixture. Toss quickly and thoroughly. Serve tuna tartare on a small plate and drizzle remaining sauce around the plate.

Serves 8

VINNY'S ON WINDWARD

CHEF BRIAN KIBLER

Vinny's on Windward thrills diners with innovative and fresh cuisine. Chef/owners Christopher and Michele Sedgwick offer guests a dining experience that satisfies cravings in a welcoming ambiance. Chef Brian Kibler takes business lunches and pleasure dining very seriously, making sure that everyone — from large parties to a romantic dinner for two on the quiet patio — enjoys the Vinny's experience.

SPINACH, ONION AND PROSCIUTTO PIZZA

1 cup warm water, divided
1 teaspoon honey
1 package active dry yeast (2 ¼ tsp.)
3 cups flour
2 tablespoons olive oil
1 teaspoon salt
2 tablespoons white truffle oil
1 large yellow onion, julienned
2 tablespoons butter, divided
2 teaspoons fresh rosemary, minced
2 teaspoons fresh thyme, minced
2 teaspoons fresh Italian parsley, minced
1 ½ cups shaved Pecorino Romano cheese
3 cups fresh spinach, washed and stemmed
12 slices prosciutto, thinly sliced

For the dough, mix ½ cup warm (110˚) water with the honey. Stir in the yeast to dissolve. Allow to sit and proof in a warm place for 10 minutes. In a mixer fitted with a dough hook, add the flour, oil, yeast mixture and ½ cup water. Add a little more water if the dough does not form a ball. Mix on low speed for 5 minutes. Allow the dough to rest for 20 minutes. Turn the mixer back on and add the salt. Mix for another 5 minutes until the dough is smooth and firm. Remove the dough from the mixer and place in a lightly oiled bowl covered with lightly oiled plastic wrap. Allow the dough to

ACORN SQUASH TORTELLONI WITH BRAISED LAMB SHANKS

Lamb
2 tablespoons vegetable oil
3 lamb shanks
Kosher salt
Freshly ground black pepper
2 tablespoons semolina flour
2 onions, diced
6 cloves garlic, minced
2 tomatoes, peeled, seeded and diced
6 cups chicken stock
2 teaspoons rosemary, minced
1 tablespoon thyme, minced

Squash
2 acorn squash, peeled and diced
Kosher salt and pepper to taste
Pinch of grated nutmeg

Pasta
1 1/2 cups semolina flour
1/8 teaspoon salt
1 ounce water
1 egg
Egg wash (1 egg + 1 tablespoon water, beaten)

2 tablespoons butter
1 cup wild mushrooms, sliced
1/2 pound washed spinach
2 ounces grated parmesan cheese

For the lamb, in a large, heavy-bottomed Dutch oven, heat the oil. Season the lamb with salt and pepper and dust lightly with flour. Sear the lamb until all sides are well browned. Add the onion, garlic and tomato and sauté for 2 minutes. Add the chicken stock to the pan, bring to a boil then reduce the heat to a slow simmer. Simmer, covered, for 2 hours or until the meat is very tender and falling from the bone. Remove the lid and simmer until the bones and the meat separate. Remove the bones and discard. Stir and reduce until thickened. Stir in the rosemary and thyme and season to taste with salt and pepper. Keep warm until ready to serve.

For the squash, preheat oven to 300°. Peel, seed and dice the squash. Season with salt, pepper and nutmeg. Spread on a lightly greased sheet pan and bake for 45 minutes, or until soft and completely cooked through. Remove the squash from the oven and rice using a food ricer or food mill. (If you don't have one, use a potato masher and mash until all lumps are removed.) Return the squash to the oven to "dry," about 15 more minutes. Chill until ready to use.

For the pasta, place the semolina flour and salt in a large mixing bowl. Make a well in the center. In a 1-cup measuring cup, measure 2 tablespoons water and combine with the egg. Pour this into the well in the flour and stir with a fork until a dough comes together. Add a little more water as needed just to form the dough. Dump the dough onto floured work surface and knead for 5 minutes to develop the gluten. The dough should be shiny when you have kneaded enough. Divide the dough into 2 pieces, cover and let rest for 20 minutes. Feed one piece of dough through a pasta machine on the thinnest setting. If you don't have a pasta machine, roll on a floured surface until very thin. Cut the pasta into 4" circles using a very large biscuit cutter. Cover with a damp towel and refrigerate until ready to use.

To make the tortelloni, working in small batches, lay out the pasta circles and brush with egg wash. Place a small spoonful of the squash in the center of each pasta round. Fold the circle in half and firmly press the edges together. The egg will act as a glue. Be careful not to get any of the squash mixture in the seam. Make sure the seams are completely closed. Bring both ends of the half circle together around your finger and press very firmly to stick together. Repeat with remaining pasta. Place on a lightly floured sheet pan and cover with a damp cloth until ready to cook.

In a large pot, bring 2 quarts of water to a rolling boil. Melt the butter in a large sauté pan. Gently sauté the mushrooms for about 4 minutes. Boil the tortelloni for 3 minutes. Drain and gently toss in with the mushrooms. Quickly toss in the spinach and season with salt and pepper. Remove from the heat. Place a large spoonful of the lamb into a large, flat bowl. Spoon some of the tortelloni over the top and sprinkle with the parmesan cheese.

Serves 6

GEORGES BANK HADDOCK WITH OREGANO-FENNEL COUSCOUS

Couscous

1 cup water
1 cup couscous, quick cooking
1 tablespoon olive oil
½ teaspoon salt
2 tablespoons butter
½ fennel bulb, shaved thin
2 heirloom tomatoes, cut into wedges
1 sprig oregano, picked

Marjoram Vinaigrette

2 ounces extra virgin olive oil
2 ounces Champagne vinegar
1 shallot, minced
1 sprig marjoram, picked
Salt and freshly ground black pepper to taste

Haddock

2 ounces vegetable oil
Kosher salt and freshly ground black pepper
2 pounds haddock fillets with skin, bones
   removed, cut into 4 pieces
Flour for dusting
2 lemons, quartered

For the couscous, combine the water, olive oil and salt in a medium-sized saucepan. Bring to a full boil. Stir in the couscous and turn off the heat. Cover and let stand for at least 5 minutes. Uncover and fluff the couscous with a fork.

For the vinaigrette, in a blender place all of the ingredients and blend on high until completely emulsified.

Preheat oven to 500°. To cook the haddock, put vegetable oil in a hot sauté pan. Generously season both sides of the haddock with salt and pepper. Lightly dust the fish in flour. Place fish in hot oil, flesh-side down, for 2 minutes or until golden brown. Turn fish over and add lemon wedges to the pan. Place pan into oven for 2-3 more minutes.

To finish couscous, in a sauté pan melt 2 tablespoons butter and add fluffed couscous. Add the shaved fennel and heirloom tomatoes and season with salt and pepper. Cook for 1-2 more minutes and turn off the heat. Add the oregano. Drizzle half of the vinaigrette over the couscous mixture.

Serve the haddock on a portion of the cooked couscous. Drizzle plates with remaining vinaigrette.

Serves 4

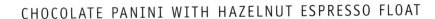

CHOCOLATE PANINI WITH HAZELNUT ESPRESSO FLOAT

1 vanilla bean
1 quart half and half
1 cup hazelnuts, toasted and ground
10 egg yolks
1 cup sugar
¼ cup Frangelico (hazelnut-flavored liqueur)

12 ounces bittersweet chocolate, chopped
12 slices rustic country sourdough bread
6 cups brewed espresso, hot

For this recipe you will need an ice cream machine.

Cut the vanilla bean in half and scrape the tiny beans into a nonreactive saucepan. Add the scraped pod to the mixture. Add the half and half and the hazelnuts. Scald the mixture and cover with plastic wrap. Allow to steep in the refrigerator overnight. Remove from the refrigerator and strain through a fine mesh strainer. Heat just until steaming. In a separate bowl, beat the egg yolks with the sugar. Stir some of the hot cream mixture into the yolks to temper. Slowly stir in the remaining cream. Stir in the Frangelico. Return to the refrigerator and chill until very cold. Freeze ice cream according to manufacturer's directions for the ice cream machine.

For the panini, preheat oven to 450°. Divide the chopped chocolate into 6 portions. Sprinkle over 6 slices of bread. Make a sandwich by placing the extra slices of bread on top of the chocolate. Toast for 5-10 minutes, or until the chocolate is melted and toast is crisp and browned.

Cut the sandwiches in half on the bias. Scoop the hazelnut ice cream into an oversized coffee cup. Pour hot espresso over the ice cream. Arrange 2 halves of the panini around the float and enjoy dipping the panini into the float.

Serves 6

METROTAINMENT BAKERY

PASTRY CHEF BARB PIRES

Metrotainment Bakery Pastry Chef Barb Pires waves her magic whisk as she creates an extensive menu of over 40 varieties of cakes and pies. These homemade, mouthwatering desserts can be savored by the slice at any of parent company Metrotainment Cafes' restaurants, including Einstein's, Joe's on Juniper, Cowtippers, Cheyenne Grille and Garrison's Broiler & Tap. Situated in Atlanta's popular Midtown area, Metrotainment Bakery also caters social and business functions.

RED VELVET CAKE

Cake
Oil
¾ cup butter
1½ cups sugar
3 eggs
⅜ cup red food coloring
¼ cup cocoa
15 ounces cake flour
1½ teaspoons baking soda

1½ tablespoons white vinegar
1½ cups buttermilk
1½ teaspoons vanilla

Cream Cheese Frosting
8 ounces unsalted butter, cold
8 ounces cream cheese, cold
14 ounces 10X powdered sugar
1 teaspoon vanilla

Preheat oven to 350°. For the cake, spray the bottom and sides of 2 9" cake pans with oil. Line the bottom of the pans with wax paper or parchment and spray the paper. Cream the butter and sugar in a mixer with the batter beater on medium speed. Add eggs one at a time, beating well after each addition. Scrape the bowl often. Make a paste of the red food coloring and cocoa and add to batter. Change mixer speed to low and alternately add flour and buttermilk, starting and ending with flour. Add vanilla. Dissolve the baking soda in the vinegar in a 1-cup measure, as it will foam up. Add to cake batter. Scrape the bowl to ensure even blending and divide batter between prepared cake pans, smoothing the tops. Give each pan a sharp rap on the counter to dislodge any air bubbles. Bake for 40 minutes, or until tester comes out clean. Remove cakes from oven and let cool in pan for 10 minutes. Remove from pan and continue to cool on wire rack.

For the frosting, cream butter in mixer with batter beater until smooth. Add cream cheese and continue beating on low speed until mixture is smooth. Gradually add powdered sugar, scraping sides and bottom of bowl often. Beat in vanilla and continue to mix until frosting is of spreading consistency. Place bottom layer of cake on cake plate and frost top. Place second layer on top of first and frost sides and then top of cake. Store cake in a cool place until serving time. Refrigerate any leftovers.

Serves 10

PUMPKIN CHEESECAKE

Crust

2½ cups crushed gingersnaps
1 cup ground pecans
¼ cup butter, melted

Cheesecake

2 pounds cream cheese
1½ cups sugar
6 eggs
2 teaspoons vanilla
2 teaspoons cinnamon

2 teaspoons ground ginger
1 teaspoon ground cloves
2 cups canned pumpkin

Topping

½ cup light brown sugar
⅓ cup light corn syrup
¼ cup butter
1 tablespoon vanilla
½ cup chopped pecans

Preheat oven to 300°. Butter a 10" springform pan. Place an oblong pan filled with water in the oven on the shelf below the shelf the cheesecake will be baked on.

For the crust, put gingersnaps in a food processor and process to fine crumbs. Mix crumbs, ground pecans and butter and press mixture on bottom and sides of prepared springform pan.

For the cheesecake, beat cream cheese and sugar on low speed until smooth. Add eggs one at a time, beating well after each addition. Add vanilla. Reserve 1 cup of the mixture at this point. With the mixer on low speed, blend the spices and pumpkin purée into the remaining mixture. Pour this pumpkin-cream cheese mixture into prepared crust. Then spoon in the reserved plain cream cheese mixture to create a marbling effect.

Bake the cheesecake for 50 minutes. Turn the oven off and leave the cheesecake in the oven overnight. Remove cake from oven and chill for 4-6 hours.

For the topping, combine sugar, corn syrup and butter in small saucepan. Cook over medium heat, stirring constantly, for approximately 5 minutes, or until sugar is dissolved. Stir in vanilla. Add pecans and stir to mix. Cool mixture to room temperature. Spread on cheesecake. Refrigerate until serving time.

Serves 16

COCONUT CREAM PIE

1½ cups crushed vanilla wafers
½ cup almonds, toasted and ground fine
½ stick butter, melted
4 eggs
½ cup cornstarch
4 cups half and half
1 cup sugar
2 teaspoons vanilla
¼ teaspoon salt
1 tablespoon butter
4 cups unsweetened shredded coconut
2 cups whipping cream
½ cup powdered sugar
¼ cup unsweetened shredded coconut, toasted

For crust, combine vanilla wafer crumbs, almonds and butter. Press mixture on bottom and up sides of 9" pie plate and set aside.

Combine eggs and cornstarch in bowl and whisk until thoroughly mixed.

In a heavy 6-quart saucepan, bring the half and half, sugar, vanilla and salt to a boil and scald (rises to top). Whisk ½ cup of scalded half and half into egg-cornstarch mixture. Quickly add egg mixture into the rest of the scalded half and half and whisk rapidly. Cook until very thick, about 3 minutes. Remove from heat and stir in butter and shredded coconut.

Fill the prepared crust, mounding the filling mixture, and refrigerate for at least 4 hours.

Whip cream slightly and then add powdered sugar and continue to whip until soft peaks form. Top pie with whipped cream. Garnish with toasted coconut.

Serves 8

IRISH SODA BREAD

¼ pound butter
1 cup sugar
6 ⅝ ounces all-purpose flour
1 teaspoon baking soda
¼ teaspoon salt
1 cup buttermilk
1 cup raisins
1 cup walnuts, broken into large pieces

Nonstick baker's spray

Preheat oven to 300°. Spray a loaf pan with nonstick spray.

Cream butter and sugar in mixing bowl using the batter beater on low speed. Scrape the sides of the bowl to ensure blending. Combine flour, baking soda and salt in a small bowl. Alternately add these dry ingredients and buttermilk to butter-sugar mixture, beginning and ending with dry ingredients. Scrape down the mixture. Add raisins and walnuts. Mix until just combined. Scoop and pat dough into prepared pan, spreading to corners of pan.

Bake for 1 hour 25 minutes. Test for doneness. Inside temperature should reach 180° on an instant-reading thermometer.

Serves 6 to 8

CHOCOLATE MIDNIGHT TORTE

Cake
Oil
7 ¾ ounces cake flour
3 cups sugar
1 cup cocoa
½ teaspoon salt
1½ cups butter, melted
6 eggs
1 tablespoon vanilla extract

Chocolate Ganache
8 ounces semi-sweet chocolate
½ cup heavy cream

Chocolate Truffles
2 ounces unsweetened chocolate
2 tablespoons butter
1¼ cups 10X powdered sugar
¼ cup heavy cream
Fresh raspberries
Fresh mint

Preheat oven to 325°. For the cake, spray the bottom and sides of a 10" springform cake pan with oil. Line the bottom of the pan with wax paper or parchment and spray the paper. Place the flour, sugar, cocoa and salt in a mixing bowl and whisk on low speed until completely blended. Add the melted butter and scrape the sides of the bowl to ensure blending. Add all the eggs at once. Add vanilla. Scrape the bowl again but do not over-mix. Pour batter into prepared pan. Bake for 1 hour. Remove cake from oven and let cool to room temperature in the pan.

For the ganache, put semi-sweet chocolate and heavy cream in a microwave-safe bowl. On low power, microwave mixture for 2 minutes. Check mixture and microwave again for 1 minute, or until chocolate is all melted. Make sure microwave is on low power, as chocolate will seize if melted at too high a temperature. Mix melted chocolate and cream together until well blended and smooth. Spread on top of cooled cake.

For the truffles, melt chocolate in microwave according to directions above. Mix butter and powdered sugar in mixer on low speed. Add melted chocolate and heavy cream and mix until smooth. Spoon mixture into a pastry bag fitted with a star tip and pipe rosettes on top of cake. Top each truffle with a raspberry and a mint leaf.

Serves 12

PHILIPPE'S BISTRO

CHEF PHILIPPE HADDAD

Tucked in the cozy Peachtree Hills neighborhood, Philippe's Bistro enchants with a delectable mixture of French and Belgian cuisine served in a charming atmosphere. Led by revered chef/owner Philippe Haddad, this dining destination boasts an exhibition kitchen, lively bar and popular second-story, climate-controlled patio — all lending to its reputation as a fine dining experience.

WATERCRESS RISOTTO WITH MORELS, SPRING PEAS AND GRILLED QUAIL

2 bunches watercress, well washed and trimmed
1 cup water
Coarse salt
Freshly cracked black pepper
6 cups chicken stock
¼ cup butter, divided
1 cup finely diced onion
½ cup panchetta, julienned (optional)
1 cup dry white wine
2 cups aborio rice
2 tablespoons celery, diced and blanched
2 tablespoons carrots, diced and blanched
2 tablespoons leeks, diced
1 cup fresh spring peas
½ pound morel mushrooms
¼ cup shallots, minced
8 boneless quail
1 tablespoon olive oil
2 tablespoons fresh thyme, stemmed and chopped
Fresh thyme sprigs for garnish

Blanch watercress in boiling water for 15 seconds and immediately drain and refresh under cold running water. Pat dry. Place the watercress and 1 cup cold water in a blender and purée. Season to taste with salt and pepper and set aside. Heat the stock in a saucepan and keep warm. In a separate saucepan, melt 1 tablespoon butter, add the onions (and pancetta, if desired) and sauté for 2 minutes. Add white wine and reduce by half. Add the rice and stir until coated. Add enough hot stock to just cover the rice and stir until absorbed. Continue adding hot stock a cup at a time, stirring until absorbed, until the rice is almost done but still al dente. Stir in the celery, carrots, leeks and peas. Stir in watercress purée and season to taste with salt and pepper. Cut the morels into large pieces and gently sauté with the shallots in 1 tablespoon butter for 3 minutes. Stir the mushroom sauté into the risotto. Stir in the remaining butter until melted.

For the quail, preheat oven to 325°. Cut the wing tips from the quail. Rub the quail with olive oil and season the birds with thyme, salt and pepper. Sear the quail in a hot sauté pan until browned. Finish cooking and keep warm in oven.

Cut the legs from the quail. Serve a large spoonful of the risotto in the center of a plate. Split and butterfly the quail on top of the risotto. Garnish with a fresh sprig of thyme.

Serves 8

BELGIAN-STYLE MUSSELS WITH HOEGAARDEN BEER

2 pounds mussels
2 stalks celery, diced
½ cup shallots, minced
½ cup mixed fresh herbs, minced (parsley, thyme, cilantro, etc.)
¼ teaspoon curry powder
8 tablespoons unsalted butter
⅓ cup Hoegaarden beer
½ cup fish stock (optional)
⅓ cup heavy cream (optional)
Kosher or sea salt
Freshly ground white pepper

Clean mussels and trim the beards. Make sure all of the mussels are still closed. Discard any opened mussels. Sauté the celery, shallots, herbs and curry powder in the butter until the shallots are translucent. Add the mussels and cover for 5 minutes. Add the beer, fish stock, cream and stir in pan until mussels are completely coated. Cook a few more minutes just until all of the mussels have opened. Season with salt and pepper.

Serve in a deep, flat bowl with the juices. These are excellent accompanied by some pommes frites.

Serves 4

DIVER SCALLOPS AND CAULIFLOWER VELOUTÉ
WITH CEPES AND TRUFFLES

2 pounds diver scallops (fresh, large 10-12 count per pound)
1 head cauliflower, cooked soft and diced
8 tablespoons butter, divided
1 bunch leeks, white part only, washed and cut into large dice
1 carrot, peeled and diced
6 shallots, minced and divided
¼ cup + 2 tablespoons flour
¼ cup + 2 tablespoons sherry
2 sprigs fresh thyme
1 bay leaf
2 cups chicken stock
1 cup heavy cream
1 pound cepes (porcini) mushrooms, finely diced
2 ounces black truffle, finely diced
5 sprigs chives, sliced
Kosher salt
Freshly ground white pepper
Truffle oil

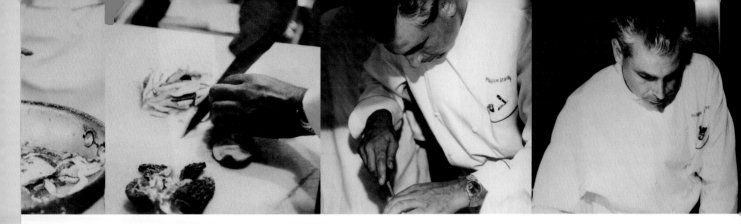

Clean and trim the scallops, trimming off the small, tough "boot." Pat dry and refrigerate until ready to use. In a large, heavy-bottomed pot, melt 5 tablespoons butter and add the diced leeks, carrots and 3 tablespoons of the shallots. Cook until vegetables are translucent and soft. In a small bowl, mix 2 tablespoons softened butter with the flour to form a paste. Stir into the sautéed vegetables. Add the scallops, cover and cook for 5 minutes. Stir in the sherry, thyme and bay leaf. Cook 4 more minutes. Slowly stir in the chicken stock, cauliflower and cream. Return to a simmer, remove from the heat and set aside. Slowly sauté the cepes, truffles and remaining 3 tablespoons shallots in 1 tablespoon butter until dry. Mixture should resemble a paste. Season to taste with salt and freshly ground white pepper. Set aside to cool. Remove the bay leaf and thyme sprigs from the scallop-cauliflower mixture and purée the mixture in a blender. Pass through a fine china cap or sieve. Mixture should be very smooth and silky. Taste and adjust seasonings with salt and white pepper as needed.

Serve in a hot soup plate or bowl. Float a spoonful of the cepes-truffle mixture on top, garnish with chives and dot with the truffle oil.

Serves 6

BACCHANALIA

PASTRY CHEF KAREN OAKLEY

Pastry Chef Karen Oakley is the mastermind behind the confectionary creations of renowned Atlanta restaurants Bacchanalia and Floataway Café. Joining the culinary dream team of creative partners Anne Quatrano and Clifford Harrison, Oakley brings an incomparable style to the Atlanta dining scene. Simple presentations belie the talent she pours into her fresh and unique dessert offerings.

BRULÉED FIGS IN CRÈME ANGLAISE
WITH RED WINE AND BLACK PEPPER SORBET

Figs
18 fresh figs, sliced in half
Turbinado sugar, for sprinkling

Crème Anglaise
1 cup heavy cream
¼ cup sugar
2 egg yolks
½ vanilla bean, scraped

Red Wine and Black Pepper Sorbet
1 bottle Cabernet Sauvignon
1 tablespoon freshly cracked black pepper
¾ cup heavy cream
1¼ cups milk
2 cups powdered sugar
5 tablespoons corn syrup

Lace Cookies
1½ cups sugar
¾ cup toasted hazelnuts, finely ground
Zest and juice of 2 oranges
¾ cup flour
½ cup melted butter

For this recipe you will need an ice cream machine.

Generously sprinkle turbinado sugar over sliced figs. Place onto a sheet pan and cook under a hot broiler for 2-3 minutes, or until caramelized.

For the crème anglaise, in a heavy-bottomed saucepan, bring the cream, vanilla and half of the sugar to a boil. Whisk the remaining sugar with the yolks. Temper the hot cream into the yolks and return entire mixture to heat, stirring constantly. Keep over low heat until mixture coats the back of a spoon. Immediately remove from heat and strain. Cool over an ice bath in the refrigerator until ready to use.

For the sorbet, in a saucepan combine wine and black pepper. Simmer for 20 minutes. Strain. Return to stove and reduce to 1½ cups. In a separate bowl, combine cream, milk, sugar and corn syrup. Temper wine into milk mixture. Cool completely. Freeze in ice cream machine according to manufacturer's instructions.

For the lace cookies, combine sugar, nuts, zest and juice. Add flour and butter, stirring until smooth. Allow to sit at least 1 hour at room temperature.

Preheat oven to 350°. On a baking sheet with a silpat, measure cookies onto sheet with a teaspoon. Bake until a deep caramel color, about 12 minutes. Allow to cool for 1 minute, then carefully lift the cookies with an offset spatula and place over a rolling pin to shape. Allow to cool completely on the rolling pin. Store in an airtight container until ready to use.

Ladle 3 ounces of the crème anglaise into the bottom of a small serving bowl. Place bruléed figs over anglaise. Place 2 lace cookies in the center to hold the sorbet. Place 1 scoop of sorbet onto cookies. Top with 1 or 2 more bruléed figs. Serve immediately.

Serves 8 to 10

DATE AND CARAMEL GALETTE WITH PARMESAN ICE CREAM

Pastry Shells
1 box Pepperidge Farm puff pastry
½ cup turbinado sugar
Flour for rolling dough

Parmesan Ice Cream
2 cups whole milk
1 cup + 1 tablespoon sugar
16 ounces parmesan rind
8 egg yolks
2 cups heavy cream

Caramel Sauce
¾ cup sugar
¼ cup water
¾ cup heavy cream

1½ cups pitted and quartered Medjool dates

For this recipe you will need an ice cream machine.

Preheat oven to 400°. Allow the frozen puff pastry to come to a working temperature. Roll out and dock pastry with a fork. Cut 12 2¾-inch circles with a cutter. Cut a 1-inch circle out of 6 of the circles. Brush uncut rounds of pastry with water and immediately top with the same diameter round with the center cut out. Brush the pastry shell with water and sprinkle generously with turbinado sugar. Bake shells for 10-15 minutes, or until sugar has caramelized and pastry is thoroughly cooked. Cool completely.

For the sauce, in a small saucepan, combine sugar and water and cook over medium heat until an amber color is achieved. Remove from heat. Slowly pour cream into caramel, stirring constantly. Be careful of splattering caramel sauce. Pour entire mixture into a metal bowl to cool.

For the ice cream, in a heavy-bottomed saucepan, heat milk and half of the sugar to almost boiling. Remove from heat, add parmesan rind and allow to steep for at least 20 minutes to incorporate the flavor. Remove rind and return milk mixture to a boil. In a separate bowl, combine egg yolks and the remaining sugar. Temper milk into yolk mixture while constantly whisking. Return the entire mixture to medium heat. Stir constantly until the mixture coats the back of a spoon. Remove and strain into cold heavy cream. Cool over an ice bath in the refrigerator. Once completely cool, freeze in an ice cream machine according to manufacturer's instructions.

In a small saucepan, heat the caramel sauce and the dates. Pour a couple of dates into each pastry shell. Pour extra caramel over shells. Serve immediately with a scoop of parmesan ice cream.

Serves 6

VALRHONA CHOCOLATE TARTS WITH CHAMPAGNE ZABAGLIONE

Tart Dough

1¼ cups flour
¼ cup cocoa powder
¼ cup sugar
¼ teaspoon salt
4 ounces cold butter
1 egg yolk
1 tablespoon water

Filling

12 ounces Valrhona chocolate, 66% bittersweet
6 ounces butter
3 whole eggs
3 egg yolks
⅓ cup sugar
¼ teaspoon salt
2 tablespoons cake flour, sifted
1 teaspoon pure vanilla extract

Champagne Zabaglione

2 egg yolks
¼ cup + 1 tablespoon sugar
½ cup dry champagne
¼ cup heavy cream

Chocolate Sauce

4 ounces heavy cream
1 ounce light corn syrup
4 ounces semi-sweet chocolate

For the dough, combine flour and cocoa powder in a small bowl and set aside. In a separate mixing bowl, cream butter, sugar and salt. Add egg yolk. Add flour mixture until just incorporated. Turn dough out onto table and finish kneading by hand. If the dough is too dry, sprinkle with water. Cover in plastic wrap and chill for at least 2 hours.

Preheat oven to 300°. When cold, roll dough out by hand onto a floured surface to ⅛-inch thick. Line 6 small tart shells. Bake for 10–12 minutes. Cool thoroughly.

For the filling, preheat oven to 325°. Over a double boiler, melt chocolate and butter. Remove from heat. In a mixer on high speed, whip eggs, yolks, sugar and salt until tripled in size. Reduce speed and gradually add flour and vanilla. Then slowly add the cooled chocolate mixture. Continue to mix until fully incorporated. Pour into prebaked tart shells. Smooth the tops and bake for 12-15 minutes or until set up.

For the zabaglione, beat the yolks and ¼ cup sugar in a stainless-steel bowl over a pot of simmering water. Continue to whip constantly by hand until mixture is thickened. Slowly add champagne and continue to whisk until you have a ribboned consistency. Remove bowl from heat and pour mixture into a mixing bowl. Whip on high speed until cool. In a separate bowl, whip the cream and remaining sugar to medium peaks. Gently fold into egg mixture. Use immediately.

For the sauce, in a small saucepan, heat cream and corn syrup. When it comes to a boil, pour over chocolate. Stir for about a minute until chocolate is completely melted and mixture is fully incorporated.

Place a warm tart on each plate. Cover half of tart with zabaglione. Garnish the plate with chocolate sauce. Serve immediately.

Serves 6

LEMON AND JASMINE ICE CREAM FLOAT WITH GINGER SYRUP

Simple Syrup
½ cup sugar
½ cup water

Jasmine Sorbet
½ cup freshly squeezed lemon juice
½ cup buttermilk
½ cup brewed Jasmine tea
½ cup simple syrup (recipe above)

Lemon Ice Cream
Juice of 10 lemons
2 cups buttermilk
2 cups heavy cream

Zest of 5 lemons
1 cup + 2 tablespoons sugar
9 yolks

Ginger Syrup
1 cup water
2 cups sugar
1 vanilla bean
½ cup candied ginger
½ cup fresh ginger, sliced
5 black peppercorns
Soda water

For this recipe you will need an ice cream machine.

For the simple syrup, in a small saucepan, bring sugar and water to almost boiling and remove from heat. Keep in the refrigerator.

For the sorbet, combine all ingredients. Chill and freeze in ice cream machine according to manufacturer's instructions.

For the ice cream, stir lemon juice into buttermilk and set aside. In a heavy-bottomed saucepan, combine heavy cream, lemon zest and half of the sugar. Bring to a boil. In a stainless-steel bowl, whisk the egg yolks and remaining half of the sugar. Temper the hot cream into the yolks. Return entire mixture to the heat, stirring constantly until thickened. Immediately remove mixture from heat and strain. Cool over an ice bath and refrigerate until cool. Freeze in ice cream machine according to manufacturer's instructions.

For the ginger syrup, combine all ingredients except soda water in a saucepan and bring to a boil. Reduce and strain.

With an ice cream scoop, place 2 scoops of lemon ice cream into a soda glass. Then place 2 scoops of jasmine sorbet on top. Mix 4 tablespoons of ginger syrup with 2 cups soda water. Pour over the ice cream. Serve immediately with a straw.

Serves 4 to 6

RASPBERRY BROWN BUTTER TARTS WITH LAVENDER ICE CREAM

Tart Dough
⅓ cup powdered sugar
7 tablespoons cold butter, cubed
2 egg yolks
1½ cups flour
2 teaspoons heavy cream

Filling
2 eggs
½ cup sugar
3 ounces butter

½ vanilla bean, scraped
1 pint fresh raspberries

Lavender Ice Cream
1 pint heavy cream
1 cup half and half
¾ cup sugar
1½ sprigs fresh lavender
½ vanilla bean
6 egg yolks

For this recipe you will need an ice cream machine.

For the dough, place powdered sugar in a mixing bowl and cut in the cold butter. Add egg yolks one at a time. Add half of the flour. Once incorporated, add the heavy cream and the remaining flour. Turn out onto a cutting board and continue to knead by hand. Form into a disc and cover with plastic wrap. Chill for 1 hour.

Roll dough out to ⅛-inch thick. Line small tart pans with dough. Freeze for 30 minutes.

Preheat oven to 325°. Bake tart dough for 25 minutes or until golden brown. Cool completely.

For the filling, preheat oven to 325°. In a large bowl, whisk together eggs and sugar. In a small saucepan, melt butter with vanilla bean scrapings. Continue cooking until butter browns and has a nutty aroma. Whisk into egg mixture.

Place some raspberries in each tart shell. Pour filling over berries. Bake for 35-45 minutes, until filling has set up. Cool completely and let sit for 2 hours.

For the ice cream, in a heavy-bottomed saucepan, heat cream, half and half, sugar, lavender and vanilla bean to a boil. In a large stainless-steel bowl, reserve egg yolks. Temper hot cream mixture into the egg yolks while constantly stirring. Place entire mixture back onto heat for 1 more minute, stirring constantly. Remove from heat and strain. Cool over an ice bath. Freeze in an ice cream machine according to manufacturer's instructions.

Place 1 scoop of ice cream on each cooled tart and serve immediately.

Serves 6 to 8

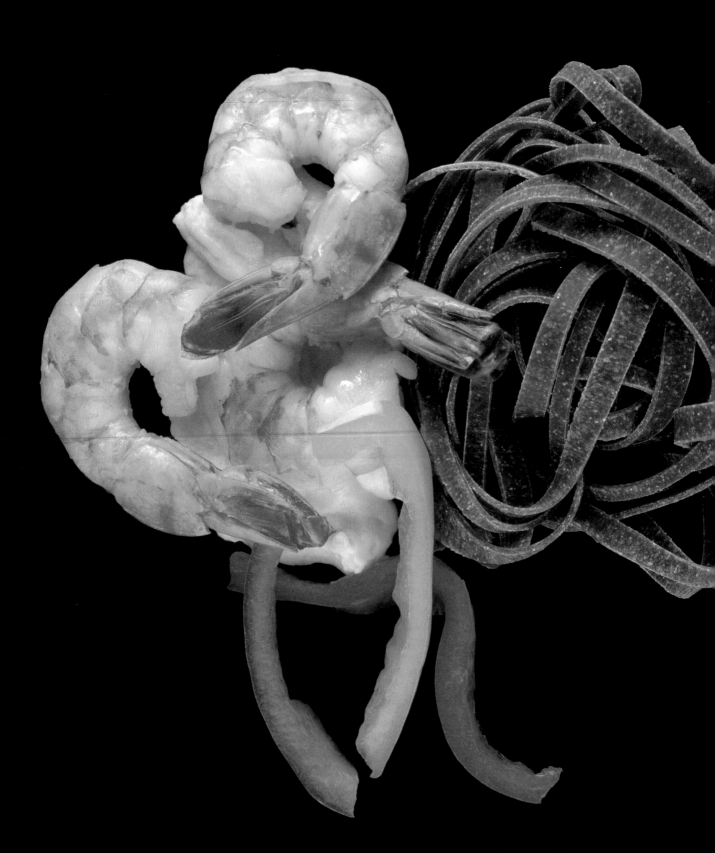

FRATELLI DI NAPOLI

CHEF JIM DUNLEVY

Fratelli di Napoli was the first restaurant in Atlanta to offer the family-style Italian dining concept of gathering a large party, ordering for the table and passing around large platters of comforting Southern Italian favorites. Chef Jim Dunlevy's authentic cooking resonates from the kitchen to the delicious platters guests share at the table.

SHRIMP AND PEPPERS IN GARLIC CREAM SAUCE

2 ounces extra virgin olive oil
1 red bell pepper, julienned
1 green bell pepper, julienned
1 yellow bell pepper, julienned
1 pound 16-20 count shrimp, peeled and deveined
2 large cloves garlic, chopped
16 ounces heavy cream
4 ounces grated Pecorino Romano cheese
½ ounce fresh basil, roughly chopped
1 pound fresh spinach linguini, cooked and drained
Salt and pepper to taste

In a large sauté pan over high heat, heat the olive oil. Add the peppers and shrimp and reduce the heat. Sauté until the shrimp are almost fully cooked, about 5 minutes. Add the garlic and cook until lightly browned. Add the cream, reduce the heat to low and simmer until cream is reduced by half. Add the cheese and stir well. Add the pasta and the basil and stir until well combined. Season to taste. Serve immediately.

Serves 6

CROSTINI ALLE OLIVE

¾ cup extra virgin olive oil, divided
10 ounces fresh mushrooms
1 garlic clove, peeled
Salt and freshly ground black pepper
6 slices firm, coarse-textured bread
½ cup black olives, pitted
6 fresh parsley leaves

Preheat oven to 350˚. Trim, wash and slice mushrooms. Heat ¼ cup of olive oil in a skillet over high heat. Add the mushrooms and whole garlic clove and sauté until mushrooms are tender, about 5 minutes. Remove the garlic clove and season with salt and pepper.

Place the bread slices on a baking sheet and drizzle with ¼ cup of the olive oil. Toast the bread in preheated oven until golden brown, about 10 minutes.

Meanwhile, process black olives in a food processor until finely chopped. Add remaining ¼ cup olive oil and process to a purée. Add this mixture to sautéed mushrooms and season with salt and freshly ground black pepper to taste.

When bread is toasted, remove from oven and spread each slice with mushroom-olive mixture. Garnish with parsley leaf and serve.

Serves 6

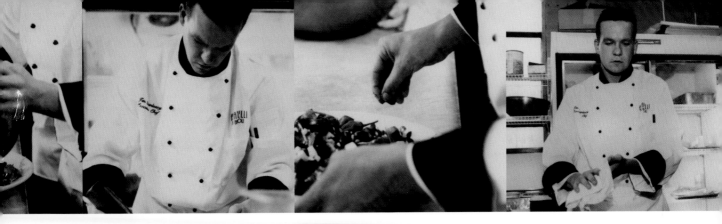

MELANZANE ALLA MOZZARELLA

2 medium eggplants, sliced into ⅜-inch rounds (12 rounds)
½ cup extra virgin olive oil
Salt and freshly ground black pepper
½ cup pesto (recipe follows)
12 slices fresh mozzarella cheese, ⅛-inch thick
3 tomatoes, sliced in ⅛-inch rounds (12 rounds)
1 bunch fresh basil

Heat grill or grill pan. Lightly brush eggplant slices with olive oil and sprinkle with salt and pepper. Grill eggplant slices until just browned and tender, about 4 minutes per side. Set on a plate.

Spread pesto on mozzarella slices and marinate for at least 10 minutes.

When ready to assemble, blot each eggplant slice to remove excess liquid and place on serving plate. Place a tomato slice on each eggplant round and then a mozzarella slice. Top each one with a fresh basil leaf. Drizzle with remaining olive oil, salt and freshly ground pepper. Refrigerate until serving time.

PESTO
4 fresh garlic cloves, minced
Salt, to taste
2 cups loosely packed fresh basil leaves
½ cup extra virgin olive oil
½ cup freshly grated parmesan cheese

Place garlic, salt and basil in the bowl of a food processor and process to a paste. Add olive oil and process again. Transfer mixture to a bowl and stir in parmesan cheese. Taste for seasoning. Store in refrigerator.

Serves 6

SWEET POLENTA WITH STRAWBERRY COMPOTE

Polenta
2 tablespoons fine dry bread crumbs
3 cups milk
½ cup sugar
1 cup finely ground white cornmeal
1 egg
4 egg yolks
4 tablespoons butter, softened
2 tablespoons finely grated lemon zest
Powdered sugar (optional)

Preheat oven to 350˚. Generously butter a 9-inch cake pan, then dust it with breadcrumbs and set aside.

Bring milk and sugar to a boil in a 6-quart saucepan. Gradually pour in cornmeal. Lower heat to a simmer and cook, stirring constantly, until mixture is very thick, about 10 minutes. Let mixture cool to lukewarm. Stir in whole egg, egg yolks, butter and lemon zest.

Spread mixture in prepared cake pan. Bake in preheated oven for 20 minutes. Turn polenta cake out onto a wire rack to cool.

Strawberry Compote
1 cup sugar
¾ cup water
1 pint strawberries, stemmed and quartered

Bring sugar and water to a boil in small saucepan and simmer for 1 minute. Remove from heat and pour over prepared strawberries. Refrigerate until serving time.

To serve, cut polenta cake into wedges and sprinkle with powdered sugar. Spoon compote on top and serve immediately.

Serves 8

RIB-EYE PIZZAIOLA

6 6-ounce rib-eye steaks
¼ cup extra virgin olive oil
1 pound tomatoes, peeled and coarsely chopped
3 teaspoons garlic, minced
2 tablespoons fresh oregano, chopped
Salt and freshly ground black pepper to taste

Preheat oven to 400°. Trim rib-eye steaks of any excess fat around edges. Heat heavy skillet over high heat and when it is hot, add olive oil and steaks. Steaks should not touch each other in the pan. Sear steaks on both sides and remove to broiler pan as they are done and place in preheated oven. Cook additional steaks in same manner, placing them on broiler pan and then in oven.

Add the tomatoes, garlic and oregano to the same hot skillet. Partially cover skillet and simmer mixture until most of liquid has been absorbed, approximately 10 minutes. Season sauce with salt and freshly ground black pepper. Remove steaks from oven and season with salt and freshly ground black pepper to taste. Plate steaks and top with sauce. Serve immediately.

Serves 6

THE FOOD STUDIO

CHEF CHRISTOPHER BRANDT

Art as food — and food as art — took center stage when The Food Studio opened in 1996 at the historic King Plow Arts Center located on the west side of Atlanta. Highlighting the cultural nature of this renovated development, The Food Studio merges culinary art with urban chic at a restaurant that's as dramatic as it is intimate. Chef Christopher Brandt leads a menu heavy on creativity but grounded in the influences of bold, American tastes.

TUNA TARTARE WITH BELGIAN ENDIVE SALAD

12 ounces sushi-grade ahi tuna, cut into small dice
2 teaspoons freshly squeezed lime juice
2 teaspoons fresh mint, minced
4 teaspoons chervil, minced, divided
   (parsley may be substituted)
2 teaspoons scallions, thinly sliced

1 tablespoon chili oil
Kosher or sea salt
1 cup Belgian endive, julienned
1 teaspoon powdered sugar
Hoisin sauce, chili oil and sprigs of chervil for garnish

For the tuna, combine the tuna, lime juice, mint, 2 teaspoons chervil, scallions and chili oil. Season with salt to taste. Cover and refrigerate until ready to serve.

For the salad, combine the endive, remaining 2 teaspoons chervil, 1 teaspoon salt and powdered sugar.

Place ¼ of the salad mix in the center of a chilled plate. Put ¼ of the tuna mixture into a 2-inch-diameter ring mold and pack tightly. Gently place the filled mold on top of the endive. Remove the mold, leaving a cylindrical tower of tuna. Garnish the plate with dots of hoisin sauce, chili oil and a sprig of chervil.

Serves 4

ARUGULA AND WATERCRESS SALAD WITH WARM BRIE DRESSING

Dressing
¼ cup dry vermouth
1 pound brie cheese, cubed
¾ cup sour cream
1 teaspoon salt
½ teaspoon freshly ground white pepper
¾ cup water, divided
5 teaspoons cornstarch
Juice of 1 lemon

Salad
½ pound arugula, thoroughly washed and stemmed
½ pound watercress, thoroughly washed and stemmed
3 tablespoons freshly squeezed lemon juice (1 lemon)
⅓ cup extra virgin olive oil
Kosher salt
Freshly ground black pepper
1 pear, d'Anjou or Bosc, stemmed, seeded and julienned
1 cup unsalted cashews, toasted

For the dressing, in a thick-bottomed saucepan, bring the vermouth to a simmer. Add the brie, sour cream, salt and white pepper. Remove from the heat and stir until the brie is melted. Strain to remove the rinds and place back on the stove. Add ½ cup water and bring to a simmer. In a small bowl, stir together the cornstarch and ¼ cup water to make a slurry. Whisk the slurry into the brie cream. Bring back to a simmer and stir until thickened. Stir in the lemon juice and adjust the seasoning with additional salt and pepper as needed.

For the salad, thoroughly wash the arugula and watercress and pat or spin dry. Mix the greens together and toss in the lemon juice, olive oil and salt and pepper to taste. Gently stuff the salad into a 3-4" ring mold. Spoon the warm brie dressing over the greens and top with pears and toasted cashews. Remove the ring and serve.

Serves 6

MAHI MAHI WITH WILTED COLLARD GREENS AND CREAMED CAULIFLOWER

Cauliflower Cream
2 tablespoons vegetable oil
½ onion, sliced
3 cups water
Salt and white pepper to taste
1 cauliflower head, chopped, divided
1 cup heavy cream
1 ounce white truffle oil

Fish
2 tablespoons oil
4 fresh mahi mahi fillets

Kosher salt
Freshly ground pepper
Juice of 1 lemon

Collard Greens
3 tablespoons butter, divided
2 cups shallots, sliced
1½ pounds baby collard greens or collard greens,
    washed, drained and julienned
¼ cup vegetable stock
2 tablespoons balsamic vinegar
Salt and pepper to taste

For the cauliflower cream, in a large, heavy-bottomed pot, heat the oil and sweat the onions until translucent. Add water, salt and pepper, and bring to a simmer. Add half of the cauliflower and cook until tender. Drain, reserving the liquid. Return cauliflower to the pot and add the cream and white truffle oil. In small batches, purée in a blender, adding the cooking liquid as needed to thin to a nice sauce consistency, about 2 cups. Season with salt and pepper to taste. Cook the remaining cauliflower in salted water until tender. Strain and fold into the creamed mixture. Keep warm until ready to serve.

For the fish, heat a sauté pan with oil and season the fillets with salt and pepper. Place the mahi mahi into the pan and do not turn or stir until golden brown. Once golden brown, flip the fish and cook the other side until golden brown. If the fish is not cooked through at this point, place it into a 350˚ oven until finished (it should be complete in just a couple of minutes). Just before serving, season the fish with lemon juice.

For the greens, heat 2 tablespoons butter in a sauté pan. Add the shallots and cook until caramelized. Add the collards, vegetable stock, salt and pepper. Toss until wilted, about 3-5 minutes. Drain and toss with the remaining butter and the balsamic vinegar just before serving.

Place a bed of greens on each plate, top with the fish and spoon some of the creamed cauliflower over the fish and greens.

Serves 4

SAVORY BUTTERNUT SQUASH AND CHEVRE PUDDING

3 cups butternut squash (about 2 medium squash)
3 teaspoons kosher salt, divided
3 eggs
1½ cups milk
¾ cup semolina flour
1 teaspoon fresh rosemary, minced
1 teaspoon fresh thyme, minced
1 teaspoon fresh sage, minced
½ teaspoon freshly ground black pepper
5 ounces chevre/goat's milk cheese
Fresh thyme, rosemary or sage sprigs for garnish

Peel, seed and dice the squash. Place in a large pot and add just enough water to cover/float the squash. Add 1 teaspoon of the salt. Bring to a boil and reduce the heat to a simmer. Cook until the squash is very tender, about 30 minutes depending on the size of the dice. Strain the cooked squash from the water and purée in a food processor until smooth. Allow to cool to room temperature. Beat the eggs and milk and stir in the semolina flour. Add the cooled squash and stir until combined. Add the herbs, remaining 2 teaspoons salt and pepper. Gently crumble in the chevre and fold to blend, being careful not to break up the crumbles.

Preheat oven to 350°. The pudding can be baked in a casserole dish (9 x 7) or in individual ramekins. Lightly oil the dish(es) and fill about three-quarters full with the mixture. Bake for about 30 minutes, or until set and golden brown on top. Baking time depends on size of dish.

Garnish with fresh thyme, rosemary or sage sprigs. This dish is a great accompaniment for roast pork.

Serves 8

VENISON OSSO BUCO

1 tablespoon kosher salt
1 teaspoon juniper berries
1 teaspoon white, pink, green and black peppercorn blend
6 venison shanks (osso buco)
¼ cup olive oil
1½ onions, peeled and chopped
1½ carrots, peeled and chopped
2 garlic bulbs, split in half so the cloves are all cut in half
¼ cup anchovies, chopped
2 cups white wine
1 lemon, juice and zest
1 cup celery, chopped
1 cup chicken stock
4 bay leaves
¼ cup fresh thyme, stemmed and chopped
3 cups canned whole tomatoes, peeled

Preheat oven to 325°. Grind the salt, juniper and peppercorns. Season venison (or other strong, tough meat you wish to braise) generously with the spice blend. Heat a heavy-bottomed roasting pan to high, add the oil, then sear the meat on all sides until nicely browned. Remove the meat and set aside. Add the onion, carrot, garlic and anchovies to the same pan. Sauté until caramelized. You may need to add a small amount of oil to the pan prior or during this process. De-glaze the pan with white wine and bring to a simmer. Add the lemon zest and juice, celery, seared shanks, chicken stock, bay leaves, thyme and tomatoes. Bring to a simmer, cover and place in oven for 2 hours, or until the meat is very tender and falling off the bone. Remove the meat from the pan and hold to the side. Strain the liquid to another pot and bring to a simmer. Periodically skim the top of the sauce, removing "scum" and any fat. Reduce until a nice, satiny sauce consistency.

Place a shank on each plate and top with the warm sauce.

Serves 6

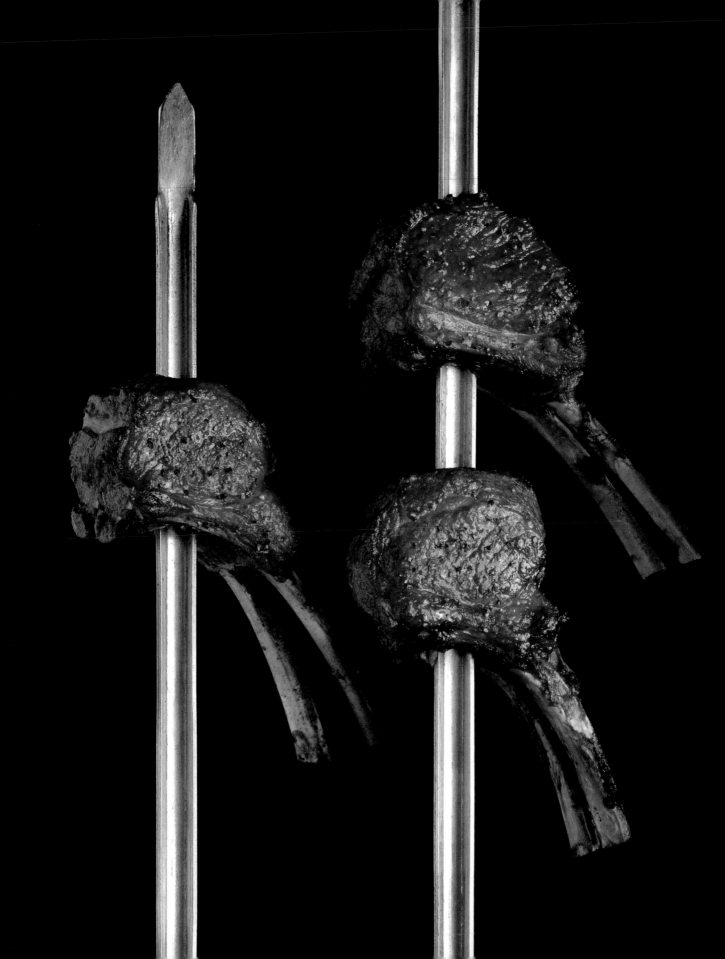

FOGO DE CHÃO

A bona fide churrascaria, Fogo de Chão (fo-go dée shown) is a genuine steakhouse from Rio Grande de Sul in Southern Brazil. Unique to Atlanta with its "Gaucho" (Southern Brazilian cowboy) waiters, delectably slow-roasted meats and spectacular exhibition of authenticity and unparalleled service, the eatery satisfies Atlantans and visitors alike in its Buckhead location.

GRILLED LAMB CHOPS
"Cordeiro Assado"

8 rib lamb chops
2 cups white wine
2 tablespoons lemon pepper
Juice of one lemon
1 tablespoon salt, or to taste
1 cup mint leaves

Vegetable oil spray
Mint jelly and mint leaves for garnish

Trim lamb of excess fat. Mix all other ingredients to make marinade, including mint leaves, and marinate lamb chops for 1 hour.

Spray grill with vegetable oil. Remove lamb chops from marinade and place on preheated grill. Grill chops without moving them for 4 minutes for medium rare. Baste chops with marinade and turn over to grill for another 4 minutes on other side. Remove to serving plate.

Season with additional salt and garnish with additional mint leaves and mint jelly.

Serves 4

CHEESE BREAD
"Pao de Queijo"

4 eggs
¾ cup corn oil
1½ cups whole milk
1 teaspoon salt
1½ cups sour tapioca flour (azedo)*
1 cup sweet tapioca flour (doce)*
¾ cup shredded parmesan cheese

Preheat a convection oven to 400° (or a standard oven to 425°). Combine all ingredients in a large bowl. Mix well until batter is smooth. Lightly grease a 12- or 24-cup mini-muffin pan or small dariole molds. Fill each muffin cup three-quarters full. Bake for 15 minutes or until golden brown. Breads should be crisp on the outside and hollow on the inside, like a popover. Serve warm.

*Sweet and sour tapioca flour can be found in Brazilian food stores.

Makes 48 to 60 Puffs

CAIPIRINHA
"Little Country Girl"

2 limes
4 tablespoons sugar
5 ounces Cachaca (Brazilian sugarcane liquor)
Ice

Wash limes and cut off ends. Slice limes in half. Remove core of limes and slice each half into 6 half-moon slices.

Mix lime slices and sugar in a cocktail shaker and smash thoroughly with a wooden stick. Add 10 or 12 ice cubes to cocktail shaker. Add Cachaca and shake well.

Pour mixture into glass filled with cracked ice and serve immediately.

Serves 4

PAPAYA CREAM
"Creme de Papaia"

1 papaya
4 scoops vanilla ice cream
1 ounce Crème de Cassis liqueur
Mint leaves

Peel and remove seeds from papaya. Cut papaya into pieces.

Put papaya pieces and ice cream in food processor and process with quick on and off pulses, just until ice cream and papaya are roughly combined.

Pour mixture into a nice goblet or brandy snifter. Garnish with Crème de Cassis and a mint leaf.

Serves 2

PORK TENDERLOIN
"Lombo"

½ bottle white wine
2 tablespoons lemon pepper
Juice of one lemon
1 tablespoon salt
Vegetable oil spray
2 pounds pork tenderloin
3 cups shredded parmesan cheese

Combine white wine, lemon pepper, lemon juice and salt in a rectangular baking dish. Trim fat and sinew from pork tenderloin and cut into slices approximately ½-inch thick. Put tenderloin slices in baking dish and marinate for 1 hour.

Preheat gas grill for 15 minutes or a charcoal grill until coals are white hot. Spray hot grill with oil and grill pork slices for 3 minutes per side. Put shredded parmesan cheese on a large plate and, as pork tenderloin comes off grill, set on top of parmesan cheese, pressing down on pork so cheese will adhere. Turn tenderloin pieces over and press parmesan cheese on other side as well. Spray grill again with oil. Place pieces of tenderloin back on grill and cook on each side until cheese melts, less than 1 minute. Cheese will become gooey and some will remain on grill. Serve immediately.

Serves 8

A R I A

CHEF GERRY KLASKALA

In the heart of Buckhead, Aria is a restaurant destined to thrive on contrasts versus concepts. Aria is the delicious vision of chef and restaurateur Gerry Klaskala. Getting to know Aria is getting to know Klaskala: serious about food, friends, art and music, and adamant that dining out be one of life's joys.

BEETS WITH GOAT CHEESE AND DILL

12 small- to medium-sized beets
4 tablespoons olive oil, divided
Kosher salt
Freshly cracked black pepper
2 tablespoons freshly squeezed lemon juice
6 ounces goat cheese, crumbled
1 shallot, minced
1 tablespoon chives, minced
2 tablespoons dill, minced

Preheat oven to 375˚. Trim and wash beets. Dry with a towel. Toss the beets with 2 tablespoons olive oil, salt and pepper. Place in a roasting pan and bake, covered, for 1-1½ hours or until tender. Allow to cool and remove skins by rubbing with a towel. Cut beets into quarters or eighths and place in a bowl. Toss with remaining olive oil, lemon juice, salt and pepper to taste. Top with crumbled goat cheese, minced shallots, chives and dill.

Serves 6

BUTTERNUT SQUASH SOUP

8 tablespoons butter (¼ lb.), divided
1 medium onion, cut into small dice
2 pounds butternut squash, peeled, seeded and cut into large dice
4 cups chicken stock
Kosher salt
Freshly ground black pepper
½ cup heavy whipping cream, whipped to soft peaks
1 tablespoon chives, minced

Preheat oven to 350°. Melt 4 tablespoons butter over medium heat in a heavy, ovenproof stock pot. Add diced onion and cook until lightly softened. Add squash and cook for 4 minutes. Add chicken stock and bring to a simmer. Cover and bake for 50 minutes or more, until squash is tender and cooked through. Allow to cool slightly and carefully purée, in small batches, in a blender. If soup is too thick, add a little more chicken stock. Whisk in remaining 4 tablespoons butter and season with salt and pepper to taste.

Warm soup bowls and ladle soup into bowls. Top with a dollop of the whipped cream and chives.

Serves 8

CHILLED GEORGIA WHITE SHRIMP WITH SILVER QUEEN CORN AND HEIRLOOM TOMATO SALAD

1 pound Georgia white shrimp, unpeeled
2 ears silver queen corn, on the cob
1 tablespoon butter
1 teaspoon ginger, minced
1 shallot, minced
1 tablespoon fresh basil, minced
2 tablespoons fresh chives, minced
2 tablespoons olive oil
2 tablespoons freshly squeezed lemon juice
2 tablespoons basil oil
Kosher salt
Freshly ground black pepper
4 large tomatoes for stuffing
2 heirloom tomatoes
2 cups mizuna or mesclun/spring mix

Boil shrimp in a pot just until pink and curled. Quickly rinse in cold water, peel, devein and cut into a large dice. Cut corn from cob and sauté in a skillet in 1 tablespoon butter until lightly caramelized, about 5 minutes. Gently toss together the shrimp, corn, ginger, shallot, basil, chives, olive oil and lemon juice in a large bowl. Season to taste with salt and pepper. Cut the top fourth off the stuffing tomatoes, carefully remove the insides, and turn upside down on paper towels to drain until ready to use. Cut the heirloom tomatoes into various shapes and sizes.

Stuff the large tomatoes with the shrimp salad. Place a stuffed tomato on the center of each plate. Toss the heirloom tomatoes with the greens, season with salt and pepper and arrange around the base of the tomato. Drizzle the basil oil over the salad and greens.

Serves 4

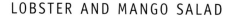

LOBSTER AND MANGO SALAD

4 1½-pound live lobsters
¼ cup + 1 tablespoon extra virgin olive oil, divided
¼ pound bacon, julienned
2 mangoes, peeled and cut into large dice
1 European cucumber, peeled, seeded and sliced
¼ cup fresh basil, julienned
2 tablespoons freshly squeezed lemon juice
Kosher salt
Freshly ground pepper
2 heads Boston lettuce, washed and patted dry
Fresh basil for garnish
Lemon wheels for garnish

In a large pot, bring 4 gallons of water to a rapid boil. Add 2 tablespoons salt and lobsters. Cook for 7 minutes. Remove lobsters and immediately plunge into ice water to stop the cooking. Allow to cool for 10 minutes. (If you are having your market cook the lobsters, ask them to steam for 7 minutes and to put on ice. They typically steam for 10-15 minutes and overcook, which makes the lobsters tough.) Remove the lobster meat from the shells by cutting down the center of the back of the shell. Wash and save the shell/tail section for serving. Remove the knuckle and claw meat. Chop the tail and knuckle meat into a large dice. Keep the claw meat intact. Wrap and refrigerate until ready to use. Heat 1 tablespoon olive oil in a sauté pan. Cook the julienned bacon until lightly crisped. Drain on a paper towel and set aside to keep warm. In a bowl, combine the lobster meat, mango, cucumber and basil. Dress with the remaining ¼ cup olive oil, lemon juice and season to taste with salt and pepper.

Arrange the lettuce leaves on the center of the plate. Spread the lobster tail shell on the plate and fill to over-flowing with the lobster salad. Sprinkle with bacon and garnish with a sprig of fresh basil and a lemon wheel.

Serves 4

ZINFANDEL-BRAISED BEEF SHORT RIBS

2 750-ml bottles zinfandel wine
2 tablespoons olive oil
8 beef short ribs
Kosher salt
Freshly cracked black pepper
2 medium onions, cut into large dice
2 carrots, peeled, cut into large dice
2 stalks celery, cut into large dice
1 leek, white part, cut into large dice
12 whole garlic cloves, peeled
6 sprigs fresh thyme
8 cups chicken stock
1 tablespoon butter

Preheat oven to 350°. Pour both bottles of zinfandel into a large saucepan, heat to a simmer and reduce by half. In a large, heavy-bottomed ovenproof Dutch oven, heat olive oil. Season short ribs generously with salt and pepper. Sear beef on all sides until browned. Remove ribs and set aside. Drain all but 1 tablespoon oil from pan. Add vegetables, garlic and thyme and cook until all are lightly browned. De-glaze the pot with the reduced wine. Add the short ribs back to the pan and fill with enough chicken stock to cover. Bring to a simmer, cover and bake for 2 hours 30 minutes, or until tender and the meat is falling from the bones. Remove the short ribs from the sauce and set aside. Skim off all fat from the braising liquid. Reheat and strain out the vegetables. Continue heating and reduce to a light sauce consistency. Add the beef short ribs and gently heat. Carefully remove the ribs to a heated platter. Season the sauce to taste with salt and pepper. Whisk in butter to finish the sauce. Serve the sauce warm with the ribs.

Serves 4

VAN GOGH'S
RESTAURANT AND BAR

CHEF EDDIE GARCIA-GUZMAN

In the quaint town of Roswell lies Van Gogh's Restaurant and Bar, offering innovative, high-quality American cuisine in an artful, cozy atmosphere. Firm believers in fresh ingredients and impeccable service, chef/owners Christopher and Michele Sedgwick have created an exceptional dining destination in Van Gogh's. Chef Eddie Garcia-Guzman takes the Sedgwick creation from the kitchen to the table.

JUMBO LUMP CRAB CAKES
WITH RED PEPPER BEURRE BLANC AND CORN RELISH

Corn Relish

1 ear sweet corn

$\frac{1}{3}$ cup red bell pepper, cut into small dice

$\frac{1}{3}$ cup green bell pepper, cut into small dice

$\frac{1}{4}$ cup red onion, cut into small dice

$\frac{1}{4}$ teaspoon kosher salt

$\frac{1}{4}$ teaspoon freshly ground black pepper

Beurre Blanc

$\frac{1}{3}$ cup shallots, minced

$\frac{1}{3}$ cup red bell pepper, diced

1 cup champagne vinegar

$\frac{1}{2}$ cup heavy cream

8 tablespoons unsalted butter

$\frac{1}{4}$ teaspoon kosher salt

$\frac{1}{4}$ teaspoon white pepper

Crab Cakes

1 pound jumbo lump crabmeat

2 tablespoons flour

$\frac{1}{4}$ teaspoon kosher salt

$\frac{1}{4}$ teaspoon white pepper

$\frac{1}{4}$ teaspoon cayenne pepper

$\frac{1}{4}$ cup heavy cream

1 ounce soybean oil

For the corn relish, blanch the corn until cooked through and cut the kernels from the cob. Place corn in a bowl with the diced peppers and onions and toss with the salt and pepper. Taste and adjust seasoning with salt and pepper as needed. Set aside.

For the beurre blanc, place the shallots, red peppers and vinegar in a nonreactive saucepan. Cook over medium-high heat until liquid is reduced to 1 tablespoon. Add the cream and reduce by half. Remove from the heat and whisk in the butter, 1 tablespoon at a time, until incorporated into the sauce. Purée in a blender until smooth and strain through a fine mesh strainer. Season with salt and pepper to taste. Keep the sauce warm, 110° but no hotter, as it may separate.

For the crab cakes, thoroughly pick through the crabmeat, discarding any shells and cartilage that you find. Place the crab in a mixing bowl and pat dry. In a measuring cup, mix the flour, salt and peppers. Gently stir into the crab. Add the cream and gently fold into the crab mixture. Refrigerate until ready to cook.

Preheat oven to 450°. Heat the soybean oil in a nonstick pan over high heat. Divide the crab mixture into desired cake size and place into the hot oil. (An ice cream scoop works well.) Cook the crab cakes until golden and turn in the pan. Place the pan in the oven and finish cooking until golden, about 5 minutes. Remove the crab cakes from the oven and place onto serving plates. Top with the beurre blanc and some corn relish.

Serves 4 to 6

RUSTIC CHICKEN BREAD SALAD

Chicken

2 whole roasting chickens
Kosher salt
Freshly cracked black pepper
4 ounces red wine vinegar, divided

Salad

1 pound arugula
8 tablespoons butter, divided
2 cups ciabatta or crusty Italian bread, cubed
1 large red onion, julienned
2 cups red pear tomatoes
¼ cup extra virgin olive oil
⅓ cup dried cranberries
Salt and pepper

Preheat oven to 450°. Trim off excess fat from the neck area of the chickens. Remove any of the organs which may be stuffed inside in a bag. Generously season the chickens inside and out with salt and pepper. Place the chickens on a rack in a roasting pan and roast for about 35-40 minutes. The chickens will not be completely cooked through at this point. If the neck bone is included with the chicken, season and roast along with the whole chickens. Remove the chickens from the oven, cut in half lengthwise, remove the backbones and reserve. Cut each half into pieces (breast, thigh, wing, drum) and set aside. Pour off the excess fat from the roasting pan and place on a stovetop burner. Heat and de-glaze the pan with half of the vinegar, scraping up any browned bits and chicken scraps in the bottom of the pan. Pour this into a large pot along with the back and neck bones and then, again, rinse the remaining liquid from the roasting pan with water, adding to the stock pot. Cover the bones with water and bring to a boil. Reduce the heat and cook down until only about ½ cup of rich stock remains in the pan, about 45 minutes. Strain the stock through a fine mesh or cheesecloth strainer. Return the chicken to the 450° oven to finish cooking and re-crisp, about 20 more minutes.

For the salad, thoroughly wash the arugula and pat or spin dry. Refrigerate to crisp until ready to use. Melt 2 tablespoons of the butter in a large sauté pan. Add the cubed bread, toss and cook on high heat to brown and crisp the croutons. When crispy, remove from the heat, season with salt and pepper and set aside. Next, heat the same sauté pan, add the remaining 2 tablespoons butter and cook the julienned onion until nicely caramelized. Add the tomatoes and sauté for 1 minute, just to heat. In a large bowl, toss the arugula with the onions, tomatoes, croutons, dried cranberries, remaining vinegar, ½ cup warm stock and olive oil. Season to taste with salt and pepper.

Divide the salad among the plates. Top with the crispy chicken.

Serves 4

TEQUILA-CURED SALMON GRAVLAX WITH CORIANDER FLATBREAD

Gravlax

1 pound kosher salt
1 pound brown sugar
¼ cup tequila
1 side salmon, skin on, fillet
2 medium beets, sliced very thin
½ bunch fresh cilantro, minced
½ bunch fresh dill, minced

Crème Fraîche

½ cup sour cream
½ cup heavy cream

Habañero Pepper Jam

⅓ cup yellow bell pepper, diced
⅓ cup red bell pepper, diced
⅓ cup poblano pepper, diced
⅓ teaspoon habañero pepper, minced
2 green onions, minced
½ cup red onion, cut into small dice
1 shallot, minced
1 teaspoon ginger root, grated
3 tablespoons sugar
½ teaspoon kosher salt
1 teaspoon sesame oil
2 tablespoons cilantro, minced
2 tablespoons freshly squeezed lime juice

Flatbread

1 teaspoon caraway seeds
1 teaspoon fennel seeds
1 teaspoon coriander seeds
1 teaspoon sesame seeds
1 tablespoon kosher salt, divided
2 cups flour
1 ½ tablespoons sugar
2 eggs, divided
½ cup milk
1 teaspoon butter

The gravlax needs to be started 3 days prior to serving. In a small bowl, mix together the brown sugar, salt and tequila. Equally and uniformly pat onto all sides of the salmon. Lay the salmon, skin-side down, in a shallow, nonreactive pan. Arrange the beet slices on the top, overlapping to cover the entire top of the salmon. Cover the beets with the minced cilantro and dill and pat down. Cover the gravlax with plastic wrap and place a pan of the same size on top. Weight down with clean bricks or filled cans. Wrap again in plastic wrap. Refrigerate for 72 hours. To finish the gravlax, gently scrape away the marinade and slice the salmon very thinly, across the grain, at a 45˚ angle from the skin. Discard the skin. Carefully place the sliced gravlax on a clean pan covered with plastic wrap, wrap and refrigerate until ready to use.

The crème fraîche needs to be started 2 days prior to serving. Whip the heavy cream to soft peaks. Fold the cream into the sour cream. Cover with plastic wrap and leave at room temperature for 24 hours. Stir the thickened mixture, cover and refrigerate until ready to use.

For the habañero pepper jam, over high heat, sauté the peppers, onions, ginger, salt and sugar in sesame oil for 4 minutes. Add the lime juice to the peppers and reduce until very thick and syrupy. Finish with cilantro.

For the flatbread, preheat oven to 350˚. Mix caraway, fennel, coriander, sesame and 1 teaspoon of kosher salt in a small bowl. Set aside. In a mixer fitted with the paddle, mix the flour, sugar and 2 teaspoons salt. Beat one egg with the milk and add to the flour mixture. Add the butter and continue to mix until a soft dough forms, about 4 minutes. Allow the dough to rest for 5 minutes. Divide the dough into two pieces and, using a rolling pin, roll out on a lightly floured surface into a very thin oval sheet. Transfer dough to a lightly oiled baking sheet. In a small bowl, beat the remaining egg with 1 tablespoon water. Brush over dough and sprinkle with the seed mixture. Bake until brown and crispy, about 10-15 minutes.

Break the flatbread into large pieces, about the size of a cocktail napkin. Place a piece of the flatbread on a plate, place two slices of the gravlax on top of the flatbread, top with a dollop of crème fraîche and then a small spoon of the habañero jam. Repeat another layer of all.

Serves 8

GRILLED MAHI MAHI WITH WARM HABAÑERO PICO DE GALLO

Pico de Gallo
2 tablespoons leek, white part only, diced
¹/₃ cup yellow bell pepper, diced
¹/₃ cup red bell pepper, diced
¹/₃ cup green bell pepper, diced
¹/₄ cup poblano pepper, finely diced
1 teaspoon habañero pepper, finely diced
¹/₂ cup yellow onion, diced
1 clove garlic, minced
1 teaspoon ginger root, grated
Olive oil
1 roma tomato, seeded and diced
2 tablespoons cilantro, chopped
2 tablespoons light brown sugar
2 teaspoons orange juice
Salt and freshly ground black pepper

Polenta
3 ears corn, grilled
4 cups chicken stock
1 cup stone-ground cornmeal
¹/₄ cup + 2 tablespoons heavy cream
¹/₂ cup parmesan cheese, grated

Mahi Mahi
6 mahi mahi fillets, about 4 ounces each
2 tablespoons olive oil
Kosher salt
Freshly ground white pepper

For the pico, sauté the leeks, peppers, onion, garlic and ginger in olive oil for 5 minutes. Add the tomato, cilantro, brown sugar and orange juice and simmer for 2 minutes. Add salt and pepper to taste. Set aside and keep warm.

For the polenta, cut the grilled corn off the cob and set aside. In a large saucepan, bring the chicken stock to a boil. Using a stiff wire whisk, slowly stir in the cornmeal. Continue stirring until the cornmeal is cooked through, about 8 minutes. Stir in cream and cheese and season to taste with salt and pepper. Fold in the grilled corn. Keep warm until ready to serve.

For the fish, season the mahi mahi with a brush of olive oil and salt and pepper. Grill on a hot grill, 2 minutes per side, or until just cooked through but still moist.

Spoon out a large portion of the polenta onto each plate, place a piece of the mahi mahi on top and spoon warm pico over the top.

Serves 6

ROAST PORK WITH GOAT CHEESE BREAD PUDDING

Pork
4 cups apple cider
½ cup bourbon
½ cup brown sugar
2 sprigs rosemary
2 tablespoons whole black peppercorns
2 tablespoons salt
4-5-pound boneless pork loin
2 tablespoons flour
2 tablespoons oil

Bread Pudding
½ pound unsalted butter, divided
1½ loaves rustic bread, crusts removed
2¼ cups milk
4 large eggs
1½ teaspoons salt

2 dashes Tabasco sauce
12 ounces fontina cheese, grated
6 ounces goat cheese, crumbled
6 ounces (about 1 cup) parmesan cheese, grated

Sauce
½ cup shallots, sliced thin
½ cup red wine vinegar
½ cup brown sugar
½ cup red wine
2 cups veal or beef stock
2 black plums, seeded and sliced thin
2 tablespoons Chambord (black raspberry liqueur)
1 tablespoon unsalted butter
Salt and pepper to taste

Fresh rosemary sprigs for garnish

For the pork, mix the cider, bourbon, sugar, rosemary, salt and pepper together. Place in a glass bowl or large Ziploc bag along with the pork loin and marinate, refrigerated, for 24 hours.

Preheat the oven to 325°. Remove the pork loin from the marinade and pat dry. Lightly dust the loin with flour. Heat a large sauté pan with 2 tablespoons oil and sear the pork until well browned on all sides. Transfer the pork to a roasting rack in a roasting pan and cook for about 1 hour, or until 145° in the center. Remove from oven and let rest 15 minutes before slicing.

For the bread pudding, prepare a large ovenproof casserole dish by buttering the inside bottom and sides. Slice the crustless bread into ½-inch-thick slices. Butter each slice on one side. In a bowl, beat the eggs and add the milk, Tabasco and salt. Set aside. Place one layer of bread, buttered-side up, in the bottom of the casserole. Sprinkle a layer of each of the cheeses over the top and repeat with the bread and cheeses. Pour the egg mixture over the bread and cheese. Set aside for 1 hour. When ready to cook, preheat oven to 350°. Bake for 45 minutes, or until golden brown and bubbly.

For the sauce, in a heavy-bottomed saucepan add shallots, wine, vinegar and sugar. Heat to a simmer and reduce by two-thirds or until syrupy, so the liquid coats the back of a spoon (this will only take about 5 minutes). Add the stock and reduce again by half. Add the Chambord and sliced plums and cook for another 2 minutes. Finish the sauce by whisking in the butter. Taste and adjust seasoning with salt and pepper.

Spoon the warm bread pudding onto the serving plates. Slice the pork loin across the grain and serve on top of the bread pudding. Finish with the plum sauce and a sprig of rosemary.

Serves 8

FLOATAWAY CAFÉ

CHEF DE CUISINE GREG DUNMORE

Sister restaurant of the renowned four-star Bacchanalia, Floataway Café celebrates the fruit of the earth and the joy of the seasons. A commitment to local flavors and fresh, organic produce is evident in its menu. Tucked in an industrial strip in a renovated warehouse, the restaurant pays homage to the peasant, European-style cuisine favored by chefs and creative partners Anne Quatrano and Clifford Harrison. Chef de Cuisine Greg Dunmore executes their vision, producing distinct, regional flavors.

PAN-SEARED SALMON WITH WILTED LEEK AND CUCUMBER SALAD

Salad
4 leeks, trimmed and diced
2 European cucumbers, peeled, seeded and diced small
¾ cup champagne vinegar
½ cup finely diced shallots
4 tablespoons sugar
1 tablespoon Dijon mustard
1 tablespoon chopped fresh chervil or curly parsley
2 tablespoons extra virgin olive oil
Salt and pepper to taste

Pan-Seared Salmon
1 teaspoon olive oil
6 6-ounce pieces of salmon
Sea salt
Freshly cracked black pepper
1 lemon, freshly squeezed
1 tablespoon fresh chives, chopped

In a pot of boiling water, blanch leeks for 1 minute and cool in an ice-water bath. Chill in the refrigerator. Lightly salt cucumbers and allow to drain for 1 hour. In a large bowl combine vinegar, shallots, sugar, mustard and chervil. Whisk together, slowly drizzling in olive oil until emulsified. Season to taste. Squeeze out excess liquid in leeks and cucumbers and combine with the vinaigrette.

In a nonstick pan, heat oil until almost smoking. Season salmon on both sides with sea salt and pepper. Sear in the pan about 1-2 minutes per side. If thick fillets, place in a 400° oven for about 5 to 7 minutes to finish them. Squeeze lemon juice over cooked salmon. Serve over a bed of the wilted leek and cucumber salad. Garnish with chives.

Serves 6

ALMOND TART WITH FIG PRESERVES

Fig Preserves
1 pound figs
1 pound sugar

Tart Dough
⅔ cup powdered sugar
7 ounces butter, softened
2 egg yolks
3 cups flour
2 tablespoons heavy cream
¼ teaspoon salt

Almond Filling
1 cup butter, softened
1 cup + 2 tablespoons sugar
3 eggs
8 ounces blanched almonds, toasted and ground fine
¼ teaspoon salt

Cut off top stems and then halve the figs. Combine with sugar and allow to sit covered overnight.

In a mixing bowl, cream butter, sugar and salt until light and fluffy. Add yolks one at a time. Add 1½ cups of flour and mix until incorporated. Add heavy cream and the rest of the flour until incorporated. Remove from mixer and bring together by hand into a disc shape. Wrap in plastic wrap and refrigerate for 1 hour.

Preheat oven to 325°. Grate dough into 11-inch tart shell and press to cover the sides and bottom. Place in the freezer for 30 minutes. Bake until golden brown, about 12 minutes. Cool completely.

Cook the fig-sugar mixture slowly in a saucepan over low heat for 1 hour or until syrup is thickened.

For the filling, preheat oven to 325°. In a mixing bowl, cream butter and sugar until light and fluffy. Add eggs, one at a time, and ground almonds and salt. Spoon almond filling over cooled tart shell until completely covered. Bake for 35 minutes or until completely set up. Serve with warm fig preserves.

Serves 8 to 10

ROASTED MARINATED BEETS

Beets

2½ pounds medium-sized beets, washed with tops (greens) removed
¼ cup raspberry vinegar
1½ tablespoons butter
2 tablespoons honey
Salt and pepper to taste

Vinaigrette

½ cup red wine or raspberry vinegar
¼ cup honey
3 shallots, finely diced
½ cup grape-seed oil
Salt and pepper to taste

Preheat oven to 350°. Place washed beets in a deep roasting pan. Fill pan halfway up the beets with water. Add vinegar, butter, honey and salt and pepper. Cover tightly with aluminum foil and roast for 2–3 hours, or until a knife goes easily into a beet's center. Remove from oven and remove beets from cooking liquid. Wearing gloves, peel off the exterior skin of the beets and dice.

For the vinaigrette, place vinegar and honey in a bowl and whisk together. Add shallots and, while slowly whisking, add the grape-seed oil in a thin stream. Season with salt and pepper and toss with the warm, peeled and diced beets.

*The beets will be even better the second day.

Serves 6 to 8

MAINE LOBSTER WITH SWEET CORN AND FINGERLING POTATOES

3 1–1¼-pound live lobsters
1 teaspoon olive oil
1 shallot, finely diced
1 carrot, finely diced
1 stalk celery, finely diced
4 ears of sweet corn, kernels cut from cob
1 pound fingerling potatoes, peeled, diced and blanched
1 cup reduced chicken stock
2 tablespoons sweet unsalted butter
1 teaspoon fresh tarragon, chopped
Salt and pepper to taste

Poach lobsters in a large pot of boiling water for 6 minutes. Remove lobsters and run under cold water to cool. Crack shells and pull out lobster meat. Reserve the meat in the refrigerator. In large sauté pan, heat the olive oil and add shallot, carrot, and celery. Sauté until wilted, add corn and potatoes and cook for 2-3 minutes, until slightly golden. Add ½ cup of the chicken stock. Bring to a simmer and add 1 tablespoon butter and salt and pepper to taste. Remove from heat and season with chopped fresh tarragon.

In a saucepan over medium-to-low heat, heat lobster meat slowly in the remaining ½ cup chicken stock and 1 tablespoon butter.

Divide the corn mixture into 6 bowls and top each with half a lobster.

Serves 6

SLOW-ROASTED PORCHETTA WITH FRESH PEAS

1 fresh ham, bone in with skin intact, cured for 3 days in salt water
  (1 cup salt per 1 gallon cold water. Change water daily and keep refrigerated.)
¾ cup toasted fennel seeds
1 tablespoon crushed red pepper
8 cloves garlic, peeled
1 tablespoon kosher salt
1 cup freshly squeezed lemon juice, divided
1½ cups olive oil
4 cups fresh shelled peas
2 shallots, finely diced
Salt and pepper

Preheat oven to 500°. Remove ham from brine and let dry. Cut slices through the skin and fat just to the meat, about 1 inch apart. In a food processor, combine fennel seeds, red pepper, garlic and salt and pulse until roughly chopped. Press this spice mix into the slits cut into the ham.

Place ham in a roasting pan and cook for 45 minutes to 1 hour. Turn oven down to 250°. Combine ½ cup lemon juice with 1 cup olive oil and pour over the ham. Continue to cook for about 10 hours. If your ham is small, cooking time will be shortened. After this much time, the meat should be falling off the bone. (You may also cook it overnight at 225° for 12 hours.)

In a pot of boiling water, blanch peas and transfer to an ice-water bath to stop cooking. In a small bowl, whisk the remaining lemon juice and olive oil with the shallots. Season with salt and pepper. Drain peas and mix in vinaigrette. Slice ham and serve with pea vinaigrette.

> Servings vary according to size of ham. This amount of vinaigrette and peas serves 4 to 6.

GARRISON'S
BROILER & TAP

CHEF GLENN MILLS

Garrison's Broiler & Tap is a traditional restaurant offering great steaks and seafood. Chef Glenn Mills lends great influence to the extensive menu and prepares all the meat on "classic" steakhouse broilers. This Duluth restaurant boasts a raw bar, spacious patio and cigar and martini bar located on the roof. With a 1920s New York steak saloon atmosphere, Garrison's is a city favorite with timeless appeal.

PECAN-CRUSTED FLOUNDER WITH TOMATO-SCALLION LEMON BUTTER

Flounder
2 cups pecans, chopped in a food processor
1½ cups all-purpose flour
1 teaspoon salt
4 whole flounder sides
Olive oil

Butter
1 large tomato, cut into ¼-inch dice
¼ pound butter
Juice of 2 lemons
5 tablespoons scallions, chopped
2 tablespoons parsley, chopped

For the flounder, mix together pecans, flour and salt and firmly pat both sides of fish fillets with this flour mix. In a hot pan coated with olive oil, sauté flounder 2 minutes on each side or until golden brown.

For the butter, place tomato dice, butter and lemon juice in a medium sauté pan and heat until butter is melted. Add scallions and parsley and then spoon over fish.

Serves 4

BLUE CRAB AND FRIED GREEN TOMATO NAPOLEON
WITH RED PEPPER VINAIGRETTE

Crab

1 pound blue crabmeat, picked to remove shell
1 teaspoon Old Bay seasoning
4 teaspoons fresh dill, chopped
½ teaspoon salt
4 tablespoons butter, melted

Tomatoes

2 large green tomatoes, cut into 8 ½-inch slices
1 cup flour, seasoned with salt and pepper
4 eggs, beaten
4 cups cornmeal, seasoned with salt and pepper
Olive oil

Vinaigrette

3 red bell peppers
¼ cup red-wine vinegar
¼ teaspoon salt
¾ cup olive oil

Diced yellow bell pepper and fresh dill for garnish

Mix all crab ingredients well and set aside.

Dredge tomato slices in flour, then place in beaten eggs. Coat well in eggs, then dredge in cornmeal to coat nicely. Set tomatoes aside.

For the vinaigrette, preheat oven to 400˚. Roast peppers in oven until skin begins to separate from the pepper. Remove peppers from oven and place in a covered container until cool. Peel, seed and rinse the peppers. In a food processor or blender, place peppers, vinegar and salt. Turn mixer on and slowly pour in olive oil until vinaigrette is well blended. Set aside.

To Assemble

In a large sauté pan coated with olive oil, fry green tomato slices over medium heat. Heat until golden brown and tender inside. Drain on cloth or paper towel. In another sauté pan, heat crab mixture until just warm.

To finish each portion, place 1 tomato slice on plate. Top with approximately 2 tablespoons crab mixture. Place another slice of tomato on top of crab and spoon on another 2 tablespoons crab mixture to form two layers. Drizzle generously with red pepper vinaigrette. Garnish with a little sprinkle of diced yellow pepper and a sprig of fresh dill.

Serves 4 to 6

SAUTÉED SHRIMP WITH SAVANNAH RICE

Rice
4 strips bacon, julienned
1 yellow onion, diced
1¾ cups rice
2 medium tomatoes, diced
1 cup water
2 cups tomato juice
1 teaspoon salt

Shrimp
2 tablespoons olive oil
24 large shrimp, peeled and deveined
Salt and freshly ground black pepper to taste
4 tablespoons butter
4 teaspoons garlic, minced
4 tablespoons scallions, chopped

Garnish
4 strips bacon, cooked very crisp and chopped
2 tablespoons parsley, chopped

In a medium saucepot, add bacon and onions. Cook slowly on medium heat until onions begin to brown, being careful not to burn. Add rice, tomatoes, water, tomato juice and salt. Cover and cook over medium heat until done, about 30–45 minutes. Set aside and keep warm.

In a medium sauté pan, heat olive oil and sauté the shrimp. Season with the salt and pepper while cooking. When shrimp are almost cooked through, add butter, garlic and scallions. Remove from heat.

Place a generous amount of the rice onto 4 plates. Spoon shrimp and butter over rice, dividing evenly.

Sprinkle each plate with some of the chopped bacon and parsley and serve.

Serves 4

SEARED BEEF FILET WITH WILD MUSHROOM MASHED POTATOES
AND BLUE CHEESE-PORT WINE BUTTER

Butter
½ pound butter, softened
6 ounces crumbled blue cheese
¼ cup port wine, any type
2 tablespoons chives

Potatoes
4 large Idaho potatoes, peeled and sliced ½-inch thick
4 tablespoons olive oil
4 cups shiitake or cremini mushrooms, cut into ¼-inch dice
½ pound butter
½ cup half and half
½ tablespoon salt
Freshly ground black pepper to taste

4 8-ounce pieces beef filet mignon
Olive oil
Salt and pepper to taste

For the butter, mix all ingredients well and set aside.

Place potatoes in a large pot of salted water and cook until fork tender. Drain well. Sauté the mushrooms in the olive oil until soft. Mash the potatoes, then mix in mushrooms and all other ingredients. Hold warm until needed.

To assemble, sear each beef filet in about 1 tablespoon olive oil to desired doneness. Season with salt and pepper.

Divide potatoes onto 4 plates and place seared filets against them. Then top with a generous amount of the blue-cheese butter. Serve immediately.

Serves 4

WARM VIDALIA ONION DIP

¼ stick butter
3 large Vidalia onions, cut into ¼-inch dice
½ cup Creole mustard
2 8-ounce packages cream cheese, softened
¼ teaspoon salt

In a large nonstick pot, melt the butter and add the onions. Slowly cook the onions on medium heat, stirring very frequently, until they begin to caramelize. This will take approximately 30 minutes.

Remove onions from pot and mix well with all other ingredients.

Should be served warm with crackers or chips of choice.

Serves 12 to 15

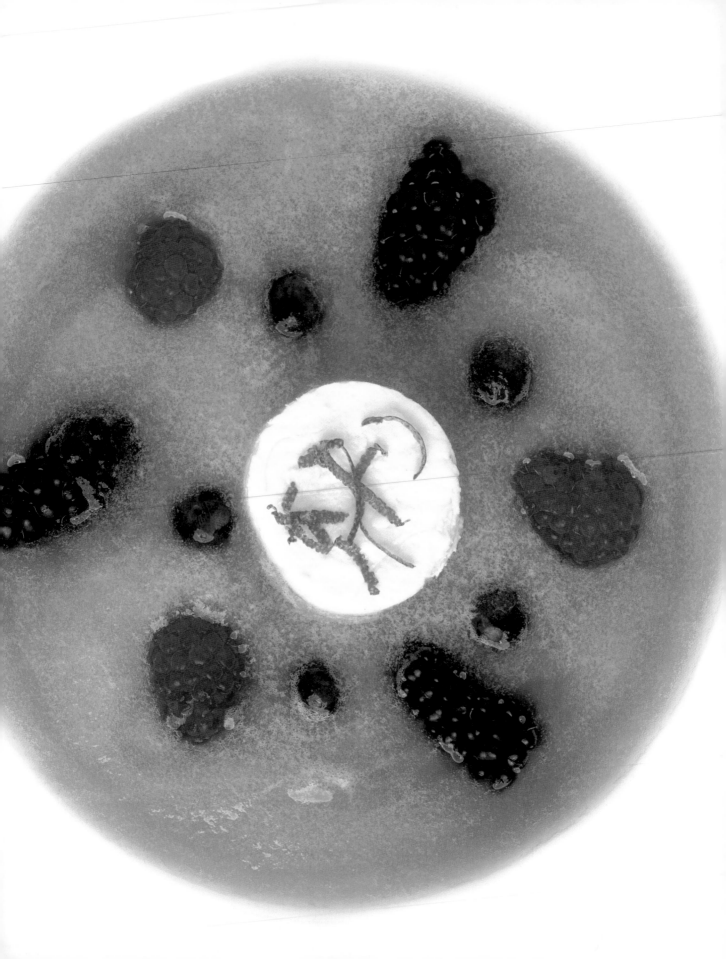

CANOE

PASTRY CHEF SARAH KOOB

Pastry Chef Sarah Koob creates unparalleled additions to a meal at Canoe with the dessert menu. Her sweet finales present Georgia's finest and freshest ingredients at their very best. One should always be warned to save room for dessert at Canoe.

GINGERED SUMMER MELON SOUP WITH KEY LIME CREAM

Ginger Root Simple Syrup
2 cups water
2 cups sugar
1 cup peeled, sliced ginger root

Key Lime Cream
1½ teaspoons gelatin
⅔ cup freshly squeezed key lime juice, divided
7 ounces sweetened, condensed milk
1½ cups heavy whipping cream

Melon Soup
¼ ripe honeydew, peeled, seeded and diced
¼ ripe cantaloupe, peeled, seeded and diced
2 cups seedless watermelon, peeled and diced
¾ cup ginger root simple syrup

Small melon dice and lime slices for garnish

For the simple syrup, boil the water and sugar until reduced by half, about 7 minutes. Remove from the heat and add the ginger root. Let steep and cool for at least 20 minutes. This mixture may be refrigerated overnight for more flavor. If storing longer, remove the ginger and store the syrup for up to 2 weeks.

For the key lime cream, in a small saucepan, soften the gelatin in 2 tablespoons cold water. Add ⅓ cup of the key lime juice and heat just enough to dissolve and melt the gelatin. Remove from the heat and stir in the condensed milk and remaining ⅓ cup of the key lime juice and let cool to room temperature. In a large bowl, whip the cream to peaks. Slowly fold in the key lime mixture. Cover and refrigerate until ready to use.

For the soup, blend melons and simple syrup until smooth. Strain if you prefer a clear soup. Chill until very cold.

Serve in an iced stemmed glass, such as a martini glass, and top with a dollop of the key lime cream, a thin slice of lime and a tiny dice of the melons.

Serves 6 to 8

BITTERSWEET CHOCOLATE BREAD PUDDING

1 pound brioche or challah/egg bread
8 tablespoons unsalted butter, melted
1½ cups sugar, divided
¾ teaspoon cinnamon
⅔ cup cocoa
1½ cups half and half
1½ teaspoons vanilla extract
4 ounces bittersweet chocolate, chopped
3 eggs
4 ounces milk chocolate, chopped

Cube the bread and toss with the butter, 1 cup of the sugar and cinnamon. Set aside. In a large pot, mix the remaining ½ cup sugar and cocoa. Stir in the half and half and vanilla and heat just to a simmer. Remove from the heat and whisk in the bittersweet chocolate until melted. Beat the eggs and temper (stir in ½ cup of the warm chocolate mixture), then add the egg mixture into the chocolate mixture. Stir all together and let cool.

Preheat oven to 325°. Mix the milk chocolate chunks into the bread mixture, then fold in the cooled chocolate mixture. Put into lightly buttered baking dish(es), either an ovenproof 9x11 glass baking dish or individual porcelain ramekins. Place in a water bath and bake for 1 hour or until butter bubbles around the edges.

Serve warm or at room temperature, however you prefer.

Serves 12

FOCACCIA

Sponge
¾ cup warm water (110˚)
2 teaspoons sugar
1 teaspoon active dry yeast
1¾ cups bread flour

Bread
1¼ cups warm water (110˚)
2 tablespoons sugar
1½ teaspoons active dry yeast
3 cups bread flour
⅓ cup olive oil
2 tablespoons kosher salt

For the sponge, dissolve the sugar in the water and then stir in the yeast. In a mixer with a dough hook, mix the flour into the yeast mixture. Let this mix until a good dough develops with a nice smooth skin. Remove and put in a lightly oiled bowl, cover with an oiled piece of plastic wrap and refrigerate overnight. This should expand to double in size.

For the bread, dissolve the sugar in the water and then stir in the yeast. In a mixer with a dough hook, add the sponge to the yeast mixture. Mix in the flour, oil and finally the salt. Let dough mix until it forms a nice dough with a smooth skin. Remove and let rest, covered, in a warm place for about 30 minutes. Divide dough into 2 pieces. Roll or press out onto a well-oiled baking sheet. Let this proof for 15-30 minutes until the dough springs back to the touch.

Preheat oven to 375˚. Top dough with your choice of herbs, spices or grilled vegetables and bake for 25 minutes or until brown.

Serves 6 to 8

PUMPKIN-CARDAMOM CRÈME BRULÉE

½ cup pumpkin purée
¼ cup brown sugar, lightly packed
¼ cup + 1 tablespoon sugar
½ teaspoon ground cardamom
⅛ teaspoon ground cinnamon
5 egg yolks
½ cup milk
1 cup heavy cream

Preheat oven to 325°. Mix the pumpkin purée, sugars, cardamom and cinnamon until smooth. Add the egg yolks and slowly stir in the milk and cream. Strain the mixture and pour into single-serving ovenproof ramekins. Evenly space ramekins in a water bath and bake for about 45 minutes or until set. Cover with plastic wrap and chill.

Before serving, top each with a thin coating of sugar or brown sugar and quickly "brulé" (caramelize/brown) on the top rack under a 550° broiler or with a torch.

Serves 6

CANOE'S FLATBREAD

3¼ cups high gluten or bread flour
1 cup cool water
¼ cup pepper oil, divided
2 tablespoons salt
¼ cup fresh thyme, stemmed and minced
½ cup shallots, peeled and chopped

Preheat oven to 350°. In a mixer fitted with a dough hook, mix the flour, water, 2 tablespoons pepper oil, salt and thyme. Blend, gradually adding additional small amounts of water, until a stiff dough forms. Mix for 10 minutes. Portion into 8 balls and roll each out as flat as you can get it. (A pasta machine works very well for this.) Place on a greased baking sheet and bake for 10 minutes. Take out of the oven, brush with remaining pepper oil and sprinkle with shallots. Bake for another 10 minutes, or until golden brown and crispy.

Serves 8

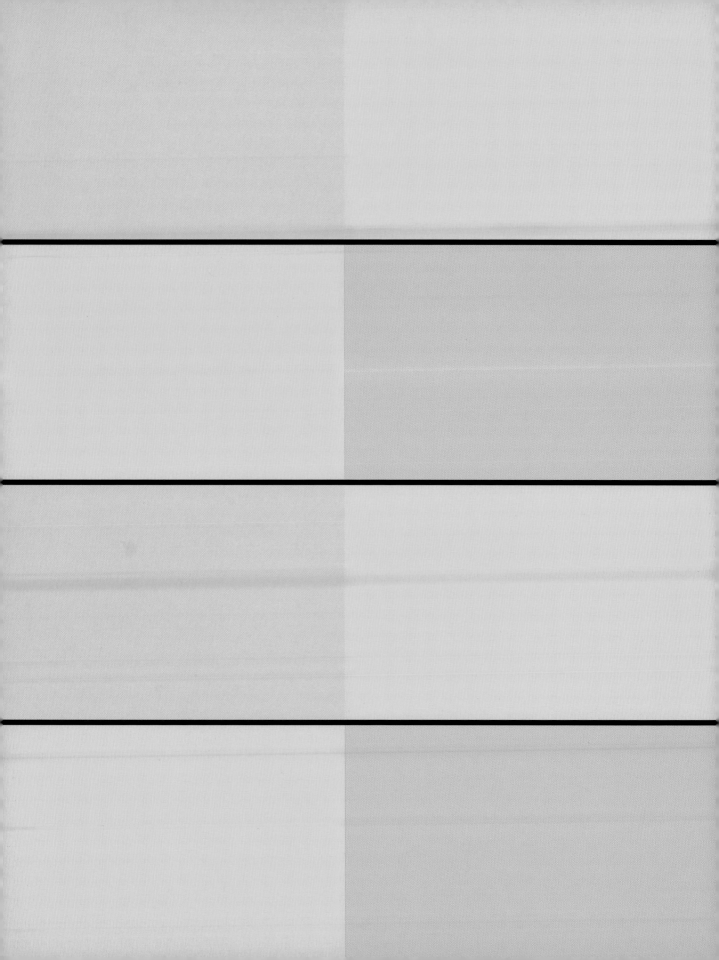

GLOSSARY OF COOKING TERMS

Brulé: Literal translation is "burn." Culinarily, to brulé is to brown/caramelize with very high heat, usually with a torch or under a broiler.

Brunoise: A very fine dice.

Chiffonade: A classic French cut, fine strips or shreds. Usually used on leaves.

Concasse: A mixture that is coarsely chopped or ground. For tomato concasse, the tomato is typically peeled, seeded and chopped fine.

Coulis: General term referring to a thick purée or sauce.

De-glaze: After a food has been sautéed and the food and excess fat have been removed from the pan, de-glazing is done by heating a small amount of liquid in the pan and stirring to loosen the browned bits of food on the bottom. The resultant mixture often becomes a base for a sauce.

Julienne: A classic French cut, a thin matchstick strip, ⅛" x ⅛", in any length desired.

Macerate: To soak a food in a liquid in order to infuse it with the liquid's flavor. A spirit such as brandy or rum is usually the macerating liquid. Marinate.

Mesclun: Also called salad mix or spring mix, it is a potpourri of young, small salad greens. Typically, a mesclun mix contains arugula, dandelion, frisee, mizuma, oak leaf, mache, radicchio and sorrel.

Mirin: A low-alcohol sweet rice wine.

Pancetta: An Italian bacon that is cured with spices but not smoked. Flavorful, slightly salty pancetta comes in a sausage-like roll.

Reduce: To boil a liquid rapidly until the volume is reduced by evaporation, thereby thickening the consistency and intensifying the flavor.

Render: To melt animal fat over low heat so that it separates from any connective pieces of tissue, which, during rendering, turn brown and crisp and are generally referred to as cracklings.

Seize: A word applied to melted chocolate that becomes a thick, lumpy mass. Seizing occurs when a minute amount of liquid or steam comes in contact with melted chocolate, causing it to clump and harden. To correct seized chocolate, add a small amount of clarified butter or vegetable oil to it, stirring until once again smooth.

Slurry: A thin paste of water and flour that is stirred into hot preparations as a thickener.

Steep: To soak dry ingredients, such as tea leaves, herbs or spices, in hot liquid until the flavor is infused in the liquid.

Sweat: A technique by which ingredients, particularly vegetables, are cooked in a small amount of fat over low heat. The ingredients are covered directly with a piece of foil or parchment paper, then the pot is tightly covered. The ingredients thus soften without browning, and cook in their own juices.

Temper: A technique by which an ingredient is stabilized through a heating process. To temper eggs, a bit of hot mixture is stirred into the eggs to warm them before adding the eggs to a larger amount of hot liquid, therefore preventing them from scrambling. Chocolate can also be tempered to prevent it from seizing.

Water Bath: To cook by placing a container of food in a large, shallow pan of warm water, which surrounds the food with gentle heat. Food may be cooked this way either in an oven or on top of the range. This technique is designed for delicate dishes, such as custards, sauces and savory mousses, in order to cook them without breaking or curdling them.

RESTAURANT LOCATIONS

Aria
490 E. Paces Ferry Road, Atlanta 30305 **404-233-7673**

Bacchanalia
1198 Howell Mill Road, Suite 100, Atlanta 30318 **404-365-0410**

Bold American Food Company
887 West Marietta Street, Studio K-102, Atlanta 30318 **404-815-1178**

Canoe
4199 Paces Ferry Road, NW, Atlanta 30339 **770-432-2663**

Fishbone Restaurant and The Piranha Bar
1874 Peachtree Rd. NW, Atlanta 30309 **404-367-4772**

Floataway Café
1123 Zonolite Road, Suite 15, Atlanta 30306 **404-892-1414**

Fogo de Chão
3101 Piedmont Road, Atlanta 30305 **404-266-9988**

Food 101
4969 Roswell Road, Atlanta 30342 **404-497-9700**

The Food Studio
887 W. Marietta Street, Studio K-102, Atlanta 30318 **404-815-6677**

Fratelli di Napoli (Buckhead)
2101-B Tula Street, Atlanta 30309 **404-351-1533**

Garrison's Broiler & Tap
9700 Medlock Bridge Road, Duluth 30097 **770-476-1962**

Hi Life kitchen & cocktails
3380 Holcomb Bridge Road, Norcross 30092 **770-409-0101**

La Tavola Trattoria
992 Virginia Avenue, Atlanta 30306 **404-873-5430**

Metrotainment Bakery
1136 Crescent Avenue, Atlanta 30309 **404-873-6307**

Philippe's Bistro
Ten Kings Circle, Atlanta 30305 **404-231-4113**

SoHo
4300 Paces Ferry Road, Suite 107, Atlanta 30339 **770-801-0069**

South City Kitchen
1144 Crescent Avenue, Atlanta 30309 **404-873-7358**

Sweet Auburn Bread Company
209 Edgewood Avenue SE, Atlanta 30303 **404-525-2253**

Theo's Brother's Bakery
12280 Houze Road, #6, Alpharetta 30004 **770-740-0360**

Van Gogh's Restaurant and Bar
70 West Crossville Road, Roswell 30075 **770-993-1156**

Vinny's on Windward
5355 Windward Parkway, Alpharetta 30004 **770-722-464**

1848 House
780 South Cobb Drive, Marietta 30060 **770-428-1848**